The Mathematics of
BANKING AND CREDIT

Table of Contents

2
The Mathematics of Ban

Part III: Credit

Support Materials

© HMH Supplemental Publishers Inc. All rights reserved.
The Mathematics of Banking and Credit, SV 9780547625614

Introduction

The **Consumer Math** series is designed to help consumers understand mathematics as it relates to their everyday lives. Activities in this series help students not only understand the underlying mathematical concepts and equations they encounter day to day, but also helps them to be more financially savvy.

Each workbook in the series is divided into three sections and begins with a basic review of math concepts before moving on to more specific topics. Each section includes the following: Pre-Skills Test, Problem Solving Strategies, a Review, and a Test.

In addition, each workbook includes the following support material: Group projects, Practice forms, Charts, a Glossary, and an Answer Key.

The Mathematics of Banking and Credit

The Mathematics of Banking and Credit covers the principles involved in the creation and maintenance of checking and savings accounts and lines of credit. Part I serves as a basic review of fundamental math concepts. Part II focuses on the math involved in reconciling deposits, withdrawals, and interest. Part III concentrates on the concepts involved with credit, loans, and installment buying.

Part I: Math Skills and Concepts
• Whole Numbers
• Fractions, Decimals, & Percents
• Mean, Median, & Mode
• Basic Operations on a Calculator
• Computing Mentally
• Estimating

Part II: Checking and Savings Accounts
• Checking Accounts
• Reconciling a Checking Account Statement
• Savings Accounts
• Simple & Compound Interest
• Money Tips

Part III: Credit
• Using Credit Cards
• Credit Finance Charges
• Overdraft Checking
• Taking Out a Loan
• Installment Buying
• Money Tips

4

Comprehensive Lessons

A **Pre-Skills Test** preceding each section helps teachers evaluate students' abilities and determine learning needs before beginning the lessons.

A wide variety of relevant exercises and activities engage students and keep them interested. Examples are motivated through real-world applications. Exercises include individual skills practice, mixed practice, and application problems.

Extension features offer more challenging problems related to the lesson's theme. **Calculator** activities present problems in which using a calculator is advantageous over paper and pencil. Interesting, real-life problems in **Think About It** spur class participation and provide additional opportunities to assess students' understanding.

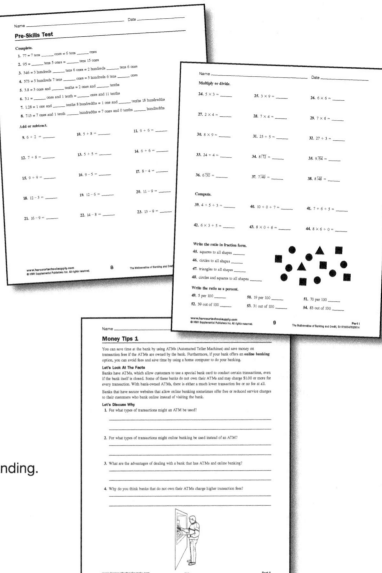

Focused review and assessment opportunities are also included for each section.

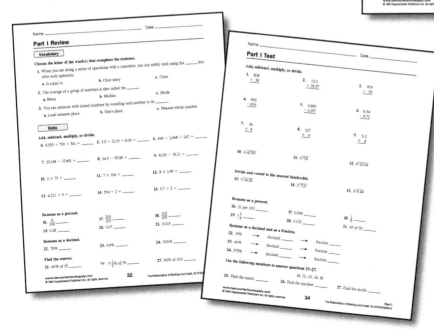

The Mathematics of Banking and Credit, SV 9780547625614

Extension Features

Money Tips examines the practical issues that affect buying decisions. Students look at factors that influence the cost of consumer goods as well as those that create consumer demand.

Mental Math helps students develop techniques to solve problems without using paper and pencil while reinforcing their confidence and estimation skills.

Estimation Skills extends students' understanding of estimation techniques and underscores their utility and practicality.

Calculator activities teach the keys and functions commonly available on calculators and emphasize the time-saving benefits.

A Strong Base in Problem Solving

Multiple **Problem Solving Applications** in each book relate math skills to people, careers, and the world around us. Applications throughout the series address consumer topics, such as renting apartments and finding miles per gallon, and careers, such as pharmacist and carpenter, which require the use of math skills.

Each **Problem Solving Strategy** presents a realistic problem, a strategy, and a step-by-step approach to solving the problem. Practice exercises reinforce the strategy. Strategies include Drawing a Diagram, Using Estimation, Using a Map, and Working Backward.

Decision Making features offer open-ended lessons that reinforce logical reasoning and move beyond computation to a consideration of factors involved in making sound decisions. Lessons in the *Consumer Math* series include Choosing Transportation, Developing a Budget, Buying Stocks, and Choosing the Correct Tax Form.

Support Materials

Group Projects

Practice Forms

Charts

Glossary

Answer Key

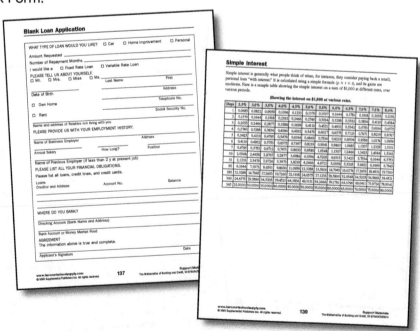

The Mathematics of Banking and Credit, SV 9780547625614

Part I:
Math Skills and Concepts

Pre-Skills Test

Complete.

1. 77 = 7 tens _____ ones = 6 tens _____ ones

2. 95 = _____ tens 5 ones = _____ tens 15 ones

3. 346 = 3 hundreds _____ tens 6 ones = 2 hundreds _____ tens 6 ones

4. 573 = 5 hundreds 7 tens _____ ones = 5 hundreds 6 tens _____ ones

5. 3.8 = 3 ones and _____ tenths = 2 ones and _____ tenths

6. 3.1 = _____ ones and 1 tenth = _____ ones and 11 tenths

7. 1.28 = 1 one and _____ tenths 8 hundredths = 1 one and _____ tenths 18 hundredths

8. 7.13 = 7 ones and 1 tenth _____ hundredths = 7 ones and 0 tenths _____ hundredths

Add or subtract.

9. $6 + 2 =$ _____

10. $5 + 8 =$ _____

11. $9 + 6 =$ _____

12. $7 + 8 =$ _____

13. $5 + 5 =$ _____

14. $6 + 6 =$ _____

15. $9 + 9 =$ _____

16. $9 - 5 =$ _____

17. $8 - 4 =$ _____

18. $12 - 3 =$ _____

19. $12 - 6 =$ _____

20. $11 - 9 =$ _____

21. $16 - 9 =$ _____

22. $14 - 8 =$ _____

23. $13 - 9 =$ _____

    The Mathematics of Banking and Credit, SV 9780547625614

Name _____ Date _____

Multiply or divide.

24. $5 \times 3 =$ _____

25. $3 \times 9 =$ _____

26. $6 \times 6 =$ _____

27. $2 \times 4 =$ _____

28. $7 \times 4 =$ _____

29. $7 \times 6 =$ _____

30. $8 \times 9 =$ _____

31. $25 \div 5 =$ _____

32. $27 \div 3 =$ _____

33. $24 \div 4 =$ _____

34. $8\overline{)72} =$ _____

35. $9\overline{)54} =$ _____

36. $6\overline{)30} =$ _____

37. $7\overline{)49} =$ _____

38. $8\overline{)48} =$ _____

Compute.

39. $4 + 5 + 3 =$ _____

40. $10 + 0 + 7 =$ _____

41. $7 + 6 + 5 =$ _____

42. $6 \times 3 + 5 =$ _____

43. $8 \times 0 + 6 =$ _____

44. $8 \times 6 + 0 =$ _____

Write the ratio in fraction form.

45. squares to all shapes _____

46. circles to all shapes _____

47. triangles to all shapes _____

48. circles and squares to all shapes _____

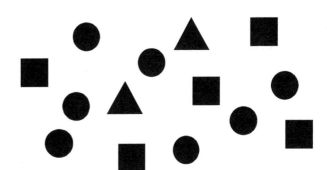

Write the ratio as a percent.

49. 5 per 100 _____

50. 19 per 100 _____

51. 70 per 100 _____

52. 39 out of 100 _____

53. 31 out of 100 _____

54. 83 out of 100 _____

Name _____   Date _____

Adding and Subtracting Whole Numbers and Decimals

Addition and subtraction are related operations.

| Addend + Addend = Sum | Sum − Addend = Addend (= Difference) |

Skill 1   Adding or subtracting whole numbers

(1a) Add 4,068 + 5,794

Step 1	Step 2	Step 3	Step 4
Add ones. Regroup.	Add tens. Regroup.	Add hundreds.	Add thousands.
$\overset{1}{}$ 4,068	$\overset{1\,1}{}$ 4,068	$\overset{1\,1}{}$ 4,068	$\overset{1\,1}{}$ 4,068
+ 5,794	+ 5,794	+ 5,794	+ 5,794
2	62	862	9,862

(1b) Subtract 8,674 − 6,319

Step 1	Step 2	Step 3	Step 4
Regroup tens. Subtract ones.	Subtract tens.	Subtract hundreds.	Subtract thousands.
$\overset{6\,14}{8,6\cancel{7}4}$	$\overset{6\,14}{8,6\cancel{7}4}$	$\overset{6\,14}{8,6\cancel{7}4}$	$\overset{6\,14}{8,6\cancel{7}4}$
− 6,319	− 6,319	− 6,319	− 6,319
5	55	355	2,355

Skill 2   Respect the position of the decimal point when adding or subtracting.

Subtract: 9.2 − 0.7

Step 1	Step 2	Step 3	Step 4
Line up the decimal points.	Write the decimal point for the difference.	Regroup ones. Subtract tenths.	Subtract ones.
9.2	9.2	$\overset{8\,12}{9\cancel{.}2}$	$\overset{8\,12}{9\cancel{.}2}$
− 0.7	− 0.7	− 0.7	− 0.7
	.	.5	8.5

> **TIP** When lining up decimals, add zero as a placeholder if necessary.
>
> Add 5.16 + 8.7 + 4.02
>
> 5.16
> 8.7**0**
> + 4.02
> _____
> 17.88

The Mathematics of Banking and Credit, SV 9780547625614

Multiplying and Dividing Whole Numbers and Decimals

Factor $\times$ Factor $=$ Product   Dividend $\div$ Divisor $=$ Quotient and (R) Remainder

$$\begin{array}{r} \text{Factor} \\ \times\ \text{Factor} \\ \hline \text{Product} \end{array}$$

$$\text{Divisor}\overline{)\text{Dividend}}\quad\text{Quotient (R) Remainder}$$

Skill 1   Multiplying whole numbers

Step 1	Step 2	Step 3
Multiply ones. Regroup.	Multiply tens. Than add 6 tens. **THINK:** 0 tens + 6 tens = 6 tens	Multiply hundreds.

$$\begin{array}{r} \overset{6}{4}07 \\ \times\quad 9 \\ \hline 3 \end{array} \qquad \begin{array}{r} \overset{6}{4}07 \\ \times\quad 9 \\ \hline 63 \end{array} \qquad \begin{array}{r} \overset{6}{4}07 \\ \times\quad 9 \\ \hline 3{,}663 \end{array}$$

Skill 2   Multiplying whole numbers and decimals

Step 1

Multiply as you would whole numbers.

$$\begin{array}{r} 1.73 \\ \times\quad 8 \\ \hline 1384 \end{array}$$

Step 2

Count the number of decimal places in the factors. There are that many decimal places in the product.

$$\begin{array}{rl} 1.73 & \text{2 decimal places} \\ \times\quad 8 & \text{0 decimal places} \\ \hline 13.84 & \text{2 decimal places} \end{array}$$

Skill 3   Dividing decimals by whole numbers

Step 1 Place the decimal point in the quotient directly above the decimal point in the dividend.

Step 2 Divide as you would whole numbers. Write additional zeros in the dividend as needed.

$$\begin{array}{r} 3.05 \\ 6\overline{)18.30} \\ \underline{18} \\ 3 \\ \underline{0} \\ 30 \\ \underline{30} \\ 0 \end{array}$$

> **TIP** Rounding the quotient:
>
> Rounding to the hundredths $0.485 \approx 0.49$
> Rounding to the tenths $0.485 \approx 0.5$
> Remember: $\approx$ means approximately equal to.

Name _____ Date _____

Practice

Add, subtract, multiply, or divide.

1. 18.5
    + 11.3

2. 4,275
    5,728
    + 982

3. 38.6
    19.8
    + 24.2

4. 5,216
    − 397

5. 78.5
    − 39.58

6. 68.21
    − 46.3

7. 242
    ×   4

8. 7.3
    × 5

9. 0.49
    ×   6

10. $4\overline{)63}$ = _____

11. $4\overline{)8.92}$ = _____

12. $6\overline{)20.3}$ = _____

13. 3,892 + 4,605 = _____

14. 1,053 + 77 + 963 = _____

15. 6.6 + 19.05 + 18 = _____

16. 847 − 615 = _____

17. 57.12 − 19.34 = _____

18. 50.08 − 29.39 = _____

19. 2 × 441 = _____

20. 5 × 0.85 = _____

21. 3 × 0.07 = _____

22. 93 ÷ 6 = _____

23. 5,285 ÷ 7 = _____

24. 17.5 ÷ 4 = _____

Divide and round to the nearest tenth.

25. 7.74 ÷ 3 = _____

26. 3.75 ÷ 6 = _____

Divide and round to the nearest hundredth.

27. 5.64 ÷ 7 = _____

28. 7.37 ÷ 9 = _____

Part I
The Mathematics of Banking and Credit, SV 9780547625614

Name _____   Date _____

Solve.

29. It is 181 miles from Austin, Texas, to Dallas, Texas, and 206 miles from Dallas to Oklahoma City, Oklahoma. How many miles is it total from Austin to Dallas and then on to Oklahoma City?

_____

30. Miranda spent $72.36 at a clothing store and $16.09 at a drugstore. How much did she spend in all?

_____

31. It is 609 miles from Ft. Worth, Texas, to El Paso, Texas. You have already traveled 93 miles. How many more miles do you need to travel? _____

32. You need to buy some school supplies. The total cost of the supplies is $99.06. You have $77.98. How much more money do you need? _____

33. It is 379 miles from Los Angeles to San Francisco. You made this trip 9 times. How many miles did you travel in all? _____

34. Your class is selling school shirts for $25 each. The class sold 15 shirts during the first hour of the sale. How much money was collected during that hour? _____

35. A 16-oz bag of lentils costs $3.84. How much is the cost per ounce? _____

36. It is about 2,178 miles from Spicewood, Texas, to Rockland, Maine. You made the trip in 6 days, traveling the same distance each day. How many miles did you travel each day? _____

Fractions, Decimals, and Percents

Skill 1   **Renaming decimals as percents**

Rename 0.9 as a percent.

Step 1	Multiply by 100 by moving the decimal point 2 places to the right. Write additional zeros if necessary.	$0.90 \longrightarrow 90.0$

Step 2	Write the percent sign.	90%

Other examples

$0.89 \longrightarrow 0.89 \longrightarrow 89\%$ $0.034 \longrightarrow 0.034 \longrightarrow 3.4\%$ $8.4 \longrightarrow 8.40 \longrightarrow 840\%$

Skill 2   **Renaming fractions as percents**

Rename $\frac{1}{5}$ as a percent.

Step 1	Write the fraction as a decimal by dividing the numerator by the denominator. Write additional zeros if necessary.	$\frac{1}{5} \longrightarrow 5\overline{)1.0}\,^{0.2}$

Step 2	Write the decimal as a percent.	$0.20 \longrightarrow 20\%$

Skill 3   **Renaming percents as decimals**

Rename 3% as a decimal.

Step 1	Divide by 100 by moving the decimal point 2 places to the left. Write additional zeros if necessary.	$3\% \longrightarrow 0.03\%$

Step 2	Remove the percent sign.	0.03

Other examples

$43\% \longrightarrow 0.43\% \longrightarrow 0.43$ $5.7\% \longrightarrow 0.05.7\% \longrightarrow 0.057$ $287\% \longrightarrow 2.87\% \longrightarrow 2.87$

Skill 4   **Renaming percents as fractions**

Rename 80% as a fraction.

Step 1 Write the percent as a fraction with a denominator of 100.

$$80\% = \frac{80}{100}$$

Step 2 Write the fraction in lowest terms.

$$\frac{80}{100} = \frac{80 \div 20}{100 \div 20} = \frac{4}{5}$$

Other examples

$$75\% = \frac{75}{100} = \frac{75 \div 25}{100 \div 25} = \frac{3}{4}$$

$$150\% = \frac{150}{100} = \frac{150 \div 50}{100 \div 50} = \frac{3}{2} = 1\frac{1}{2}$$

Skill 5   **Expressing percents as decimals**

Any percent can be expressed as a decimal.

Find 40% of 19.

Step 1 Write the problem as a number sentence.

40% of 19 is _____ ⟶ 40% × 19 = _____

Step 2 Rename the percent as a decimal.
(**THINK:** 40% = 0.40 = 0.4)

0.4 × 19 = _____

Step 3 Solve.

0.4 × 19 = 7.6

Skill 6   **Expressing percents as fractions**

Sometimes it is easier to express a percent as a fraction.

Find 75% of 16.

Step 1 Write the problem as a number sentence.

75% of 16 is _____ ⟶ 75% × 16 = _____

Step 2 Rename the percent as a fraction.
(**THINK:** 75% = $\frac{3}{4}$)

$$\frac{3}{4} \times 16 = \underline{\quad\quad}$$

Step 3 Solve.
THINK: $\frac{1}{4} \times 16 \longrightarrow 16 \div 4 = 4$

$\frac{3}{4} \times 16 \longrightarrow 3 \times 4 = 12$

$\frac{3}{4} \times 16 = 12$

So 75% of 16 is 12.

Name _____ Date _____

Practice

Rename as a percent.

1. $\frac{13}{100}$ = _____

2. $\frac{17}{100}$ = _____

3. $\frac{176}{100}$ = _____

4. 0.53 = _____

5. 0.038 = _____

6. 8 = _____

Rename as a decimal and as a percent.

7. $\frac{1}{2}$ = _____ = _____

8. $\frac{5}{8}$ = _____ = _____

9. $\frac{4}{5}$ = _____ = _____

10. $2\frac{1}{2}$ = _____ = _____

11. $8\frac{1}{8}$ = _____ = _____

12. $4\frac{3}{5}$ = _____ = _____

Rename as a decimal.

13. 23% = _____

14. 17% = _____

15. 3% = _____

16. 2.9% = _____

17. 0.06% = _____

18. 448% = _____

Rename as a fraction. Write fractions in lowest terms.

19. 60% = _____

20. 30% = _____

21. 95% = _____

22. 120% = _____

23. 177% = _____

24. 224% = _____

Find the answer. Decide whether to express the percent as a decimal or as a fraction.

25. 5% of 40 = _____

26. 50% of 24 = _____

27. 80% of 60 = _____

28. 20% of 15 = _____

29. 75% of 86 = _____

30. $33\frac{1}{3}\%$ of 63 = _____

31. $87\frac{1}{2}\%$ of 56 = _____

32. 50% of 93 = _____

33. $16\frac{2}{3}\%$ of 72 = _____

34. $37\frac{1}{2}\%$ of 84 = _____

35. 2% of 85 = _____

36. $33\frac{1}{3}\%$ of 93 = _____

The Mathematics of Banking and Credit, SV 9780547625614

Name _____ Date _____

Solve.

37. The trip between 2 towns is exactly 110 miles. You have gone 40% of this distance. How far have you gone? _____

38. Sherry received a grade of 76% on her vocabulary test. There were 25 fill-in-the-blank questions on the test. How many questions did Sherry get correct? _____

39. It takes Reggie 20 minutes to walk to school. It takes Sandy 80% of Reggie's time. How long does it take Sandy? _____

40. A used car originally was listed at $12,000. It is now being sold for 85% of its original price. How much does the car cost now? _____

41. A suit originally cost $750. It is now being sold at 40% off. How much has been deducted from the original cost of the suit? _____

42. After a taste test, 60% of the 30 people interviewed preferred a new energy bar over the previous top-seller. The rest preferred the top-seller.

    a. How many people preferred the new energy bar?_____

    b. How many people preferred the previous top-seller? _____

Problem Solving Strategy:
Interpreting Data from Tables and Graphs

Situation:

The sales staff at Donney Motors keeps records of their car and truck sales. Contests are sometimes held to encourage special efforts to sell various cars and trucks. How can these records be used to identify a salesperson's performance?

Strategy:

You can use information in a **table** or a **bar graph** to solve a problem.

Applying the Strategy:

A. The salesperson who sold the greatest number of trucks in October won a flat-screen T.V. Who was it?

THINK: Look at the column labeled "Number of Trucks Sold."

> **Step 1** Which number is the greatest?
> (22)

> **Step 2** Which name is on the same line as 22?
> (Ruth)

Ruth sold the greatest number of trucks in October and won the TV.

October Sales	
Salesperson	**Number of Trucks Sold**
Ruth	22
Art	15
John	9
Eric	12
Mindy	4

B. Eric sold the greatest number of cars and trucks last year and won a free trip. How many cars and trucks did he sell?

THINK: Look at the bar above Eric's name.

> **Step 1** Between which 2 numbers does the bar lie?
> (250 and 300.)

> **Step 2** Is the bar nearer to 250 or 300?
> (It is halfway between 250 and 300.)

> **Step 3** What number is halfway between 250 and 300?
> (250 + 300 = 550)
> (550 ÷ 2 = 275)

Eric sold 275 cars and trucks last year.

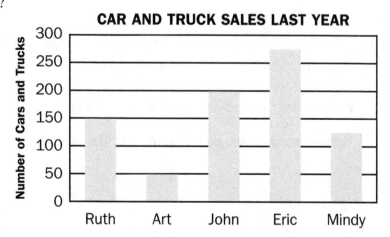

CAR AND TRUCK SALES LAST YEAR

Name _____ Date _____

Practice

Use the table of December sales for problems 1–2.

1. How many cars did Ruth sell? _____

2. How many more cars did Art sell than Eric?

   _____

December Sales	
Salesperson	**Number of Cars Sold**
Ruth	10
Art	25
John	30
Ginger	25
Eric	15
Mindy	20

The sales staff posted a bar graph to show the numbers of cars and trucks Donney Motors leased last year. Use the bar graph to answer problems 3–4.

3. How many 2-door sedans were leased? _____

4. How many more SUVs were leased than crossovers?

   _____

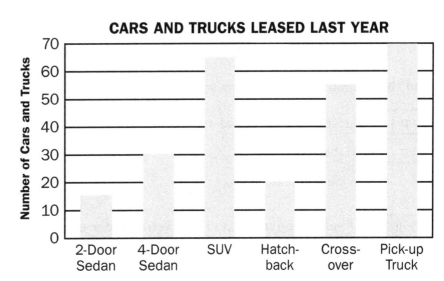

5. Use the information in the "December Sales" table at the top of the page to construct a bar graph. Use this vertical scale: 0, 5, 10, 15, 20, 25, 30, 35.

The Mathematics of Banking and Credit, SV 9780547625614

Mean, Median, and Mode

> **Mean (average)**—The sum of a group of numbers divided by the number of addends.
> **Median**—The middle number when a group of numbers is arranged in order from least to greatest.
> **Mode**—The number that occurs most frequently in a group of numbers.

Skill 1   Finding the mean

Find the mean of these basketball players' scores: 48, 36, 51, 72, 58.

| **Step 1** | Add the scores. | $48 + 36 + 51 + 72 + 58 = 265$ |
| **Step 2** | Divide by the number of scores. | $265 \div 5 = 53$ |

The mean, or average, of these scores is 53.

Skill 2   Finding the median of an odd number of scores

Find the median of these bowling scores: 126, 108, 145, 108, 117.

| **Step 1** | Arrange the scores in order. | 108   108   117   126   145 |
| **Step 2** | Find the middle score. | 117 |

The median of these scores is 117.

Skill 3   Finding the median of an even number of scores

Find the median of these bowling scores: 139, 106, 145, 113, 128, 109.

Step 1	Arrange the scores in order.	106 109 113 128 139 145
Step 2	Find the middle score. (**THINK:** There is no *one* middle number.)	113 128
Step 3	Find the mean of the two middle scores.	$113 + 128 = 241 \div 2 = 120.5$

The median of these scores is 120.5.

Skill 4   Finding the mode

Find the mode of these race times: 9.3, 9.6, 9.2, 10.2, 9.6, 10.1, 9.5.

Find the time that occurs most often.   9.6 occurs twice
The mode of these scores is 9.6.

Name _____ Date _____

Practice

Find the mean.

1. 84, 90, 96 _____

2. 5.2, 7.5, 2.6 _____

3. 162, 540, 283, 423 _____

4. 85, 53, 32, 102 _____

5. 10, 18, 16, 20, 6 _____

6. 0.28, 0.35, 0.44, 0.41, 0.27 _____

Find the median.

7. 7, 14, 25, 46, 8 _____

8. 9, 12, 8, 24, 18 _____

9. 3.3, 6.2, 9.9, 2.4, 5.6 _____

10. 2.3, 5.2, 4.7, 1.6, 4.1, 7.3 _____

Find the mode.

11. 1, 4, 5, 9, 4, 6, 7, 8

12. 9.6, 4.5, 1.7, 4.7, 6.7, 1.7, 3.2

Find the mean, the median, and the mode. Round the mean and median to the nearest tenth.

13. 66, 78, 82   mean _____   median _____   mode _____

14. 5.3, 3.5, 9.1   mean _____   median _____   mode _____

15. 402, 320, 320, 308   mean _____   median _____   mode _____

16. 65, 93, 79, 65, 74   mean _____   median _____   mode _____

17. 5.1, 2.9, 4.2, 2.9, 9.7   mean _____   median _____   mode _____

Solve.

18. Six judges scored a singing contest. For one contestant, 2 judges gave a 7.5. The other scores were 7.7, 7.9, 7.4, and 7.3. What are the mean, median, and mode of these scores?

mean _____   median _____   mode _____

Extension   **Using a Tally**

Each time Ed played miniature golf, he made a tally mark next to his score.

1. How many games did Ed play? _____

2. What are his two mode scores? _____

3. What is his median score? _____

4. What is the total of the scores of:

(a) 69? _____; (b) 68? _____; (c) 67? _____

5. What is his mean score? _____

Score	Total	Score	Total
72 - I	72	69 - ℕℐ II	
71 - I	71	68 - III	
70 - ℕℐ II	490	67 - II	

Basic Operations on a Calculator

When you want to compute quickly and accurately with greater numbers, you can use a calculator.

The four basic operations (addition, subtraction, multiplication, and division) can be performed easily.

Operation	Calculator Entry	Calculator Display
Add: 49,567 + 78,078	4 9 5 6 7 + 7 8 0 7 8 =	127.645
Subtract: 34.014 − 5.708	3 4 . 0 1 4 − 5 . 7 0 8 =	28.306
Multiply: 908 × 0.045	9 0 8 × 0 . 0 4 5 =	40.86
Divide: 4.9452 ÷ 0.078	4 . 9 4 5 2 ÷ 0 . 0 7 8 =	63.4

You can use a calculator to do a series of operations without using the [=] **key (is equal to)** after each operation.

Operation	Calculator Entry	Calculator Display
1. Subtract.	4 5 . 0 9 − 6 + Get ready to subtract.	39.09
2. Add.	4 . 7 − Get ready to subtract.	43.79
3. Subtract.	1 8 =	25.79

So, 45.09 − 6 + 4.7 − 18 = 25.79.

TIP The [CE] **key (Clear Entry)** can help you when you have entered a wrong number into the calculator.

Name _____ Date _____

Think About It

1. For which operations will the order in which you enter two numbers not affect the answer? Why?

_____

2. The entry below was made on two different calculators. One calculator displayed the answer 6.15. The other calculator displayed the answer 16.4. Explain the different answers.

$$\boxed{4}\ \boxed{.}\ \boxed{5}\ \boxed{\times}\ \boxed{3}\ \boxed{+}\ \boxed{7}\ \boxed{-}\ \boxed{8}\ \boxed{.}\ \boxed{2}\ \boxed{\div}\ \boxed{2}\ \boxed{=}$$

_____

_____

Practice

Use a calculator to compute.

1. $1{,}284{,}500 - 348{,}183 =$ _____

2. $5{,}386 + 2{,}431 =$ _____

3. $23{,}535 \div 45 =$ _____

4. $719.7 - 19.219 =$ _____

5. $426.27 \times 18.9 =$ _____

6. $45.93 \times 6.01 \div 2 =$ _____

7. 23.5 divided into $37{,}600 =$ _____

8. 0.6 divided into $0.024 =$ _____

Divide and round to the nearest tenth.

9. $17.9\overline{)389}$

10. $3.59\overline{)424}$

Divide and round to the nearest hundredth.

11. $0.29 \div 4.6 =$ _____

12. $63.8\overline{)3.567}$

Compute from left to right.

13. $724.3 - 4.281 + 375.7 - 503.18 =$ _____

14. $44.85 \div 0.2 \times 0.52 \div 15 =$ _____

Solve.

15. Jim's car odometer read 55,314 miles when he bought the car used. A year later, the odometer read 72,563 miles. How many miles had Jim put on the car in that year? _____

16. Glen ordered 500 sheets of paper. When they arrived, they formed a pile 7.2 centimeters high. How thick was each sheet? _____

Name _____ Date _____

Computing Mentally

You may often find it easier to compute mentally than to use a pencil and paper or even a calculator. You can add mentally by using numbers that are **multiples of 10** and then adjusting.

Example 1: You are buying a shirt for $19 and a jacket for $44. Mentally compute the cost of the shirt and the jacket.

Add: $19 + $44
THINK: $19 is $1 less than $20. $20 + $44 = $64

So $19 + $44 is $1 less than $64, or $63.

The shirt and the jacket will cost $63.

You can subtract mentally in the same way.

Example 2: Subtract:
  a. 94 − 18
    THINK: 18 is 2 less than 20.

    94 − 20 = 74
    So 94 − 18 is 2 more than 74, or 76.

  b. 465 − 190
    THINK: 190 is 10 less than 200.

    465 − 200 = 265
    So 465 − 190 is 10 more than 265, or 275.

Mental computation is also commonly used when you multiply or divide by **powers of 10**, such as 10, 100, or 1,000.

Example 3: Multiply: 100 × 87.30
THINK: The product must be greater than 87.3, so move the decimal point to the right.

    100 × 87.30 = 8,730
    ↑   ↑
  2 zeros |
       2 places right

Example 4: Divide: 38,430 ÷ 1,000
THINK: The quotient must be less than 38,430, so move the decimal point to the left.

    38,430 ÷ 1,000 = 38.43
     ↑   ↑
  3 places left |
       3 zeros

The Mathematics of Banking and Credit, SV 9780547625614

Name _____   Date _____

Think About It

1. Ricky argues that mental computation is a waste of time, since he has a calculator. How would you convince Ricky that he is wrong?

_____

_____

Practice Exercises

Use mental computation to add or subtract.

1. 36 + 23 = _____

2. 75 + 18 = _____

3. 267 + 519 = _____

4. 16¢ + 53¢ = _____

5. $8.21 + $1.29 = _____

6. 4.07 + 3.59 = _____

7. 77 − 36 = _____

8. 128 − 121 = _____

9. 19¢ − 13¢ = _____

10. $478 − $345 = _____

11. $1.30 − $0.41 = _____

12. 3.10 − 2.01 = _____

Use mental computation to multiply or divide.

13. 100×3.8 = _____

14. 10×0.469 = _____

15. 100×123.3 = _____

16. $13.4 \div 10$ = _____

17. $18.5 \div 100$ = _____

18. $2,992 \div 100$ = _____

Solve using mental computation.

19. A $550 patio set is marked down by $69. How much does the dishwasher now sell for? _____

20. Ten members of the marching band agree to split the $2,350.00 cost of their trip. What is each member's share? _____

Extension   **Multiplying mentally by 50 and by 25**

Multiply: 50×2.8
THINK: $100 \times 2.8 = 280$
Since $50 = 100 \div 2$, then $50 \times 2.8 = 280 \div 2 = 140$.

Multiply: 25×16.4
THINK: $100 \times 16.4 = 1,640$
Since $25 = 100 \div 4$, then $25 \times 16.4 = 1,640 \div 4 = 410$.

Use mental computation to multiply.

1. 50×74 = _____

2. 25×230 = _____

3. 50×115 = _____

Estimating Sums and Differences

A common way to **estimate** sums is to round each number to the same **place value** and then add mentally.

Example 1: About how much is the total population of Fairview County?

Town	Greenfield	Salem	Goshen	Wells
Population	21,284	3,487	38,372	10,480

Step 1 Round each number to the thousands place.

$$
\begin{array}{rcr}
21,284 & \longrightarrow & 21,000 \\
3,487 & \longrightarrow & 3,000 \\
38,372 & \longrightarrow & 38,000 \\
+\ 10,480 & \longrightarrow & +\ 10,000 \\
\hline
& & 72,000
\end{array}
$$

Step 2 Add.

72,000 is a good estimate for the total population.

Example 2:

a. Estimate: 31.07 + 0.6 + 3.87

Step 1 Round each number to the tenths place.

$$
\begin{array}{rcr}
31.07 & \longrightarrow & 31.1 \\
0.6 & \longrightarrow & 0.6 \\
+\ 3.87 & \longrightarrow & +\ 3.9 \\
\hline
& & 35.6
\end{array}
$$

Step 2 Add.

b. Estimate: 95¢ + $2.09 + $5.75

Step 1 Round each number to the ones place.

$$
\begin{array}{rcr}
\$0.95 & \longrightarrow & \$1 \\
\$2.09 & \longrightarrow & \$2 \\
+\ \$5.75 & \longrightarrow & +\ \$6 \\
\hline
& & \$9
\end{array}
$$

Step 2 Add.

The same estimating rules are used for subtraction.

Example 3:

a. Estimate: 27,387 − 2,163

Step 1 Round each number to the thousands place.

$$
\begin{array}{rcr}
27,387 & \longrightarrow & 27,000 \\
-\ 2,163 & \longrightarrow & -\ 2,000 \\
& \longrightarrow & 25,000
\end{array}
$$

Step 2 Subtract.

b. Estimate: 0.37 − 0.097

Step 1 Round each number to the tenths place.

$$
\begin{array}{rcr}
0.37 & \longrightarrow & 0.4 \\
-\ 0.097 & \longrightarrow & -\ 0.1 \\
& \longrightarrow & 0.3
\end{array}
$$

Step 2 Subtract.

Name _____ Date _____

1. How is mental computation different from estimation?

_____

_____

2. To estimate $4.80 + $2.25 + $3.40, Gail used $5 + $2 + $3 = $10. Gail's mother rounded up and used $5 + $3 + 4 = $12. What are some advantages of doing estimation the second way?

_____

_____

Practice

Estimate the sum or difference to the place value indicated.

1.   178   (hundreds)
      + 528

2.   582   (tens)
        613
       + 44

3. $8.04   (ones)
       + $3.04

4. $4.19   (ones)
         $0.35
       + $1.77

5.   597.9   (tens)
       + 77.77

6.   0.099   (tenths)
       + 0.43

7.   46,588   (thousands)
       + 8,093

8.   0.078   (hundredths)
       + 0.0088

9.   434   (tens)
       − 37

10.   86,562   (ten thousands)
        − 67,007

11. $0.45   (tenths)
        − $0.37

12. $10.32   (ones)
        − $0.64

13.   238.5   (tens)
        − 44.9

14.   7.49   (tenths)
        − 0.05

15. $695.37   (ones)
        − $5.36

Solve.

16. Johanna bought a carton of milk for $3.19. About how much change did she get from $5.00? _____

17. A jacket is advertised in a catalog for $379. The same jacket is on sale at the Clothing Outlet for $285. About how much can be saved by buying it at the Clothing Outlet? _____

Name _____   Date _____

Estimating Products and Quotients

A common way to estimate products and quotients is to round each number to its **greatest place** and then compute mentally.

Example 1: There were 285 wildlife pamphlets left to be distributed. Six friends shared the task. About how many pamphlets must each person hand out if they share the job?

| Step 1 | Round. | 285 rounds to 300. Since 6 is a 1-digit number, it does not need to be rounded. |

| Step 2 | Divide. | $300 \div 6 = 50$. |

So each person will hand out about 50 pamphlets.

Example 2:

a. Estimate: $2{,}789 \times 48$

| Step 1 | Round. | $3{,}000 \times 50$ |

| Step 2 | Multiply. | 150,000 |

b. Estimate: $22{,}270 \div 39$

| Step 1 | Round. | $20{,}000 \div 40$ |

| Step 2 | Divide. | 500 |

When multiplying or dividing decimals or money amounts, estimate by rounding each number to its **greatest nonzero place**.

Example 3:

a. Estimate: $78 \times \$0.29$

| Step 1 | Round. | $80 \times \$0.30$ |

| Step 2 | Multiply. | $24 |

b. Estimate: $324.8 \div 4.87$

| Step 1 | Round. | $300 \div 5$ |

| Step 2 | Divide. | 60 |

28

Name _____ Date _____

1. Laura calculated that 3.2 × 16.8 is 5.376. Estimate and explain why Laura's answer cannot be correct.

_____

_____

_____

Practice

Estimate the product and quotient.

1. 4,814 × 43 ≈ _____

2. 42 × $12.05 ≈ _____

3. 460 × $9.95 ≈ _____

4. 81 × 3.8 ≈ _____

5. 2.9 × 3.13 ≈ _____

6. 27.19 × 8.47 ≈ _____

7. 285 × $0.82 ≈ _____

8. 135 × 0.89 ≈ _____

9. 0.25 × 0.34 ≈ _____

10. 316 ÷ 29 ≈ _____

11. 805 ÷ 102 ≈ _____

12. $19.80 ÷ 9.6 ≈ _____

13. $23.60 ÷ 12 ≈ _____

14. $233 ÷ 43 ≈ _____

15. 87 ÷ 8.87 ≈ _____

16. 357.5 ÷ 46 ≈ _____

17. 30.7 ÷ 3.4 ≈ _____

18. 902.1 ÷ 27.5 ≈ _____

Use the menu for problems 19–20.

19. About how much will 4 juices cost? _____

20. About how many hamburgers can be bought for $10.00? _____

MENU	
Hamburgers	$2.89
Hot Dogs	$2.15
Chicken Sandwich	$3.49
Salad	$2.50
Juice	$1.19
Apple Slices	$0.79
Popcorn	$0.75

Solve.

21. Coffee mugs cost $8.75 each. About how much will 12 mugs cost? _____

22. A living room chair costs $450. About how many chairs can be bought for $1,200.00? _____

Problem Solving Strategy: Which Way to Compute?

Situation:

Suppose you are asked to find the cost of 5 pairs of socks at $1.95 a pair plus a sales tax of $0.40. Which way would you use to compute the answer?

Strategy:

Use paper and pencil skills, a calculator, or mental computation skills depending on the situation, the numbers involved, or your own personal preference.

Applying the Strategy:

Joan took out a pencil and computed: Jill took out a calculator and computed:

$$\begin{array}{r} \$1.95 \\ \times \quad 5 \\ \hline \$9.75 \\ + \quad 0.40 \\ \hline \$10.15 \end{array}$$

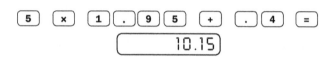

Jackie thought:

$1.95 is 5¢ less than $2. So 5 pairs are 25¢ less than $10, or $9.75, plus 40¢.

40¢ is 25¢ plus 15¢. So $9.75 plus 25¢ is $10, plus 15¢ is $10.15.

Notice that Joan, Jill, and Jackie all got the same answer.

Other Situations:

A. What is the best way to compute the amount of change that Ray received if he paid $5.00 for a $2.97 meal?

Ray can easily compute this mentally.
He thinks: $2.97 is 3¢ less than $3.00.
$5.00 − $3.00 is $2.00.

So $5.00 − $2.97 is $2.00 plus 3¢, or $2.03.

B. What is the best way for Alvin to compute the new balance in the class treasury? The balance was $357.82. He made a deposit of $182.14 and then made a withdrawal of $78.50.

Alvin needs an exact answer, and the numbers are too great to use mental computation. So he uses his calculator or paper and pencil to get $461.46.

C. What is the best way for Mr. Lee to compute the total length of pipe? One piece is $4\frac{3}{4}$ feet long, and the other is $2\frac{7}{8}$ feet long.

If Mr. Lee wants an exact answer, it is unlikely that he will use mental computation or convert to decimals and use a calculator. He will probably use paper and pencil.

$$\begin{array}{r} 4\frac{3}{4} \quad = \quad 4\frac{6}{8} \\ + \, 2\frac{7}{8} \quad = \quad + \, 2\frac{7}{8} \\ \hline 6\frac{13}{8} = 7\frac{5}{8} \text{ feet} \end{array}$$

Name _____ Date _____

1. Show how Alvin could have solved his problem with paper and pencil instead of a calculator. Discuss which method you prefer and why.

_____

_____

_____

_____

2. Show how Mr. Lee could have solved his problem using a calculator. Discuss why this answer is different from what Mr. Lee found.

_____

_____

_____

_____

Practice

Identify whether you would most likely use *paper and pencil, a calculator,* or *mental computation* to compute.

1. Find the total number of hours you worked last week. _____

2. Total three checks you are planning to deposit. _____

3. Find someone's monthly salary, based on their annual salary. _____

4. Estimate a self-employed person's quarterly taxes. _____

Use two different methods to compute. Identify the most efficient method.

5. The actual distance between two cities that are $4\frac{3}{4}$ inches apart on a map with a scale of 1 inch per 40 miles.

6. The cost per person if 19 people spent a total of $300 on a day trip.

Part I Review

Vocabulary

Choose the letter of the word(s) that completes the sentence.

1. When you are doing a series of operations with a calculator, you can safely omit using the _____ key after each operation.

   a. Is equal to   **b.** Clear entry   **c.** Clear

2. The average of a group of numbers is also called the _____.

   a. Mean   **b.** Median   **c.** Mode

3. You can estimate with mixed numbers by rounding each number to its _____.

   a. Least nonzero place   **b.** One's place   **c.** Nearest whole number

Skills

Add, subtract, multiply, or divide.

4. 9,333 + 730 + 541 = _____

5. 3.5 + 21.19 + 8.09 = _____

6. 443 + 1,048 + 247 = _____

7. 23,198 − 17,491 = _____

8. 94.3 − 65.88 = _____

9. 41.03 − 19.21 = _____

10. 2 × 73 = _____

11. 7 × 104 = _____

12. 8 × 1.99 = _____

13. 4,221 ÷ 9 = _____

14. 554 ÷ 2 = _____

15. 0.7 ÷ 2 = _____

Rename as a percent.

16. $\frac{4}{100}$ _____

17. $\frac{200}{100}$ _____

18. $\frac{215}{100}$ _____

19. 0.28 _____

20. 0.07 _____

21. 0.015 _____

Rename as a decimal.

22. 78% _____

23. 9.9% _____

24. 300% _____

Find the answer.

25. 40% of 35 _____

26. $12\frac{1}{2}$% of 36 _____

27. 90% of 300 _____

Name _____ Date _____

Use a calculator to compute.

28. $3,689 + 5,873 + 372 =$ _____

29. $58.93 \times 69.54 =$ _____

30. $4 + 40.28 - 13.239 =$ _____

31. $30.5 \times 21.12 \div 18.2 =$ _____

Compute mentally.

32. $259 + 246 =$ _____

33. $10 \times 3.9 =$ _____

34. $246 \div 100 =$ _____

35. $94,223 \div 1,000 =$ _____

Estimate.

36. $4,835 + 3,008 \approx$ _____

37. $11.89 - 2.935 \approx$ _____

38. $0.94 \times 0.47 \approx$ _____

39. $58 \div 4 \approx$ _____

40. $5\frac{2}{3} + 20\frac{1}{4} \approx$ _____

41. $7\frac{4}{5} - 3\frac{1}{3} \approx$ _____

Solve.

42. A truck driver drove 2,653 miles in April. In May, he drove 4,008 miles, and in June, 3,598 miles. What was the total number of miles that the trucker drove during these 3 months? _____

43. A textile manufacturer must finish filling an order for 5,020 yards of fabric. He has already shipped 3,950 yards. How many more yards must he ship? _____

44. Norton cut a $27\frac{3}{8}$-inch board from a board 80 ½ inches long. About how much wood is left? _____

45. Poblano peppers are on sale for $2.79 per pound. Will $10 be enough to buy 4 pounds? _____

The Mathematics of Banking and Credit, SV 9780547625614

Name _____ Date _____

Part I Test

Add, subtract, multiply, or divide.

1.   808
    + 39

2.   15.2
    + 35.97

3.   819
    + 39

4.   992
    − 839

5.   3,889
    − 1,037

6.   6.54
    − 4.72

7.   36
    × 4

8.   217
    × 9

9.   6.2
    × 8

10. $9\overline{)4{,}790}$

11. $6\overline{)7.8}$

12. $8\overline{)10.34}$

Divide and round to the nearest hundredth.

13. $3\overline{)14.29}$

14. $5\overline{)7.21}$

15. $9\overline{)8.94}$

Rename as a percent.

16. 21 per 100 _____

17. 0.066 _____

18. $\frac{1}{5}$ _____

19. $1\frac{3}{4}$ _____

20. 0.125 _____

21. 45 of 50 _____

Rename as a decimal and as a fraction.

22. 16% ⟶ decimal _____ ⟶ fraction _____

23. 40% ⟶ decimal _____ ⟶ fraction _____

24. 375% ⟶ decimal _____ ⟶ fraction _____

Use the following numbers to answer questions 25–27.

14, 12, 10, 14, 18

25. Find the mean: _____

26. Find the median: _____

27. Find the mode: _____

The Mathematics of Banking and Credit, SV 9780547625614

Name _____ Date _____

Use a calculator to compute.

28. 8,232 + 1,287 = _____   **29.** 14.7 + 0.39 + 3.05 = _____   **30.** 4,076 − 2,913 = _____

31. 50.06 − 13.29 = _____   **32.** 650.465 ÷ 7.79 = _____   **33.** 121.22 × 20.1 ÷ 305.01 = _____

Use mental computation to add, subtract, multiply, or divide.

34. 753 + 110 = _____   **35.** $813 + $509 = _____   **36.** 1.15 + 3.39 = _____

37. 29 − 21 = _____   **38.** $6.00 − $3.98 = _____   **39.** 100 × 43 = _____

40. 79.9 ÷ 10 = _____   **41.** .0011 × 1,000 = _____   **42.** 19.58 ÷ 10 = _____

Estimate.

43. 935 + 486 ≈ _____   **44.** 514 − 498 ≈ _____   **45.** $2.86 + $5.52 ≈ _____

46. 3.35 − 1.55 ≈ _____   **47.** 42 × 78 ≈ _____   **48.** 64.8 ÷ 6.2 ≈ _____

Estimate to choose the reasonable answer.

49. 66 + 54.9 + 325.4 ≈   **a.** 4.463   **b.** 466.3   **c.** 4,463

50. 5,260 ÷ 15 ≈   **a.** 3.533   **b.** 35.33   **c.** 353.3

Solve.

51. Kevin's birthday is on Saturday, and his friends are throwing him a surprise party. The total bill was $114. Six of Kevin's friends split the cost. How much was each person's equal share of the bill?
_____

52. Tomato sauce costs 89¢ per can, noodles cost $1.50 per package, grated cheese costs $1.85 per container, and baseball cards cost $2 per pack. If Thomas needs three cans of sauce, two packages of noodles, and one container of cheese, how many packs of cards can Thomas buy if he has $10?
_____

53. Helen is cutting pieces of ribbon $18\frac{1}{8}$ inches long. About how many pieces can she cut from a 20-foot length of ribbon? _____

Part II:
Checking and Savings Accounts

Name _____ Date _____

Pre-Skills Test

Write the money amount in words.

1. $48.75 _____

2. $104.50 _____

3. $279.30 _____

4. $1,483.89 _____

Compute.

5. $63.80 + $58.25 + $124.50 = _____

6. $293.84 + $53.32 + $127.03 = _____

7. $93.53 − $4.24 + $83.18 = _____

8. $530.49 − $214.96 + $430.51 = _____

9. $27.39 + $192.80 − $67.31 − $63.81 − $3.92 = _____

10. $1,943.84 − $294.73 − $97.59 − $326.16 − $27.27 + $639.20 = _____

Find the answer to the nearest cent.

11. 5% of $293.00 = _____

12. $4\frac{1}{2}$% of $374.22 = _____

13. $6\frac{1}{2}$% of $93.48 = _____

14. $5\frac{3}{4}$% of $1,200 = _____

Name _____ Date _____

Multiply.

15. $\$800 \times 0.03 \times \frac{1}{4} =$ _____

16. $\$1,500 \times 0.09 \times 2\frac{1}{2} =$ _____

17. $\$2,200 \times 0.055 \times 3 =$ _____

18. $\$840 \times 0.0675 \times 4\frac{1}{2} =$ _____

Multiply. Round to the nearest cent.

19. $\$280 \times 1.3728 =$ _____

20. $\$1,400 \times 2.5182 =$ _____

Solve.

21. How many quarter years are there in 4 years? _____

22. How many half years are there in $6\frac{1}{2}$ years? _____

23. How many months are there in $2\frac{1}{4}$ years? _____

24. How many quarter years are there in $7\frac{1}{2}$ years? _____

Find the answer.

25. $13 \times 25¢ + \$4.00 =$ _____

26. $7 \times 20¢ + \$5.00 =$ _____

27. $19 \times 15¢ + \$6.00 =$ _____

28. $9 \times 30¢ + \$7.50 =$ _____

The Mathematics of Banking and Credit, SV 9780547625614

Name _____ Date _____

Checking Accounts

The most commonly used bank account is a **checking account. Checks,** whether paper or electronic, are a convenient and safe way to make purchases and to pay bills. Checking accounts also help you keep records on when and where you spend your money.

Example 1: Suppose you wrote a check for $35.99 to pay the College Bookstore for a book. Review the parts of the check below and describe each of your entries.

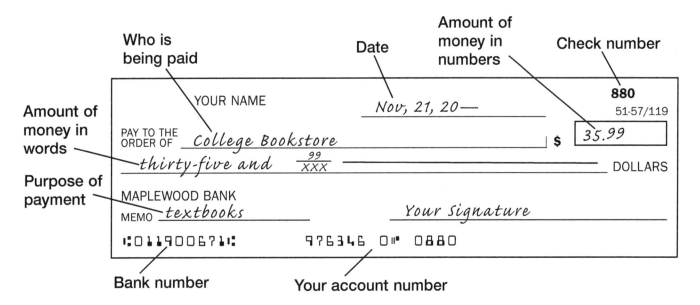

It is important that you have enough money in your checking account to cover each check that you write.

Example 2: You earned $136.00 waiting tables at the Student Union. You also had $20.00 in cash from tips. You deposited your paycheck and the cash in your checking account. Review the deposit slip below and describe each of your entries.

DEPOSIT TICKET	**CASH**	20	00	
YOUR NAME	LIST CHECKS SINGLY	136	00	
				51-57/119
DATE _November 22, 20—_				USE OTHER SIDE FOR ADDITIONAL LISTING ◀ ENTER TOTAL HERE
MAPLEWOOD BANK	TOTAL FROM OTHER SIDE			BE SURE EACH ITEM IS PROPERLY ENDORSED
ꟿ76346ꟿ	TOTAL ITEMS **TOTAL**	156	00	

CHECKS AND OTHER ITEMS ARE RECEIVED FOR DEPOSIT SUBJECT TO THE PROVISIONS OF THE UNIFORM COMMERCIAL CODE OR ANY APPLICABLE COLLECTION AGREEMENT

The Mathematics of Banking and Credit, SV 9780547625614

Name _____ Date _____

All checks and deposits should be recorded in your check register, which comes with your checks.

Example 3: You completed the check register for your check to the bookstore and for your deposit. What is your new checking account balance?

THINK: The amount of each check must be subtracted from the balance. The amount of each deposit must be added to the balance.

Review the check register below.

		RECORD ALL CHARGES OR CREDITS THAT AFFECT YOUR ACCOUNT					BALANCE	
NUMBER	DATE	DESCRIPTION OF TRANSACTION	PAYMENT/DEBIT (−)	✔ T	FEE (IF ANY) (−)	DEPOSIT/CREDIT (+)	$ 679	09
877	11/20	Dr. Sandra Stone dog's medicine	$ 15.00	$	$		− 15	00
							664	09
878	11/20	Mike's Sports Shop bowling equipment	42.00				− 42	00
							622	09
879	11/21	Atlantic Electric Co. electric bill	87.42				− 87	42
							534	67
880	11/21	College bookstore textbooks	35.99				− 35	99
							498	68
	11/22	Deposit				156.00	+ 156	00
							654	68

Your new balance is $654.68.

The Mathematics of Banking and Credit, SV 9780547625614

Name _____   Date _____

Example 4: Susan's checking account balance was $214.72. She then wrote checks for $45.77, $79.35, and $105.60. She made a deposit of $90.50. Does she have enough money in her account to pay her $78.85 electric bill?

| Step 1 | Add the deposit to the old balance.

$$\begin{array}{r} \$214.72 \\ +\ \$90.50 \\ \hline \$305.22 \end{array}$$

| Step 2 | Subtract the checks.

$$\begin{array}{r} \$305.22 \\ -\ \$45.77 \\ \hline \$259.45 \end{array}$$

$$\begin{array}{r} \$259.45 \\ -\ \$79.35 \\ \hline \$180.10 \end{array}$$

$$\begin{array}{r} \$180.10 \\ -\ \$105.60 \\ \hline \$74.50 \end{array}$$

Susan's new balance is $74.50. Therefore, she does not have enough money to cover the $78.85 electric bill.

Think About It

1. What does it mean to **bounce** a check? How can you prevent bounced checks?

_____

_____

_____

2. Why should you start writing the amount of the check in numbers and in words as close to the left as possible and add a wavy line after writing the amount in words?

_____

_____

_____

Name _____ Date _____

Practice

Remember to estimate whenever you use your calculator.

Make copies of the sample blank checks on page 132. Then write a check for each payment. Use today's date and your own name and signature.

1. Check #256 to Robert's Department Store for $38.75

2. Check #257 to The CD Outlet for $27.30

3. Check #258 to the Telephone Company for $75.42

4. Check #259 to American National Bank for $189.50

5. Check #260 to 800 Equities for $489.75

6. Check #261 to Watts Power Company for $23.69

7. Check #262 to The Bookworm for $35.50

8. Check #263 to Daily's Drugstore for $10.89

Make copies of the sample deposit slip on page 133. Then make deposit slips for the following amounts. Write the total amount of each deposit on the line.

9. A check for $145.00 and a check for $15.86

   Total deposit: _____

10. A check for $85.16 and $50.00 in cash

    Total deposit: _____

11. Checks for $29.85, $210.60, and $44.35

    Total deposit: _____

12. Checks for $48.30, $194.74, and $83.90

    Total deposit: _____

13. Checks for $239.70 and $80.53 and $120.00 in cash

Total deposit: _____

14. Checks for $82.89, $130.15, and $480.25 and $250.00 in cash

Total deposit: _____

15. Checks for $124.85, $125.76, and $133.67

Total deposit: _____

16. Checks for $243. 55 and $107.98 and $75 in cash

Total deposit: _____

Make copies of the sample check register on page 134. Make up a check register for the checking account transactions. Find the new balance.

17. Old balance: $574.83

Check: #179 to Regal Pharmacy for $25.85 on December 15
Check: #189 to Monitor Financial for $325.00 on December 18 to loan payment
Deposit: $288.92 on December 20
Check: #181 to The Toy Shoppe for $81.74 on December 22
Check: #182 to Dr. Louis Amara for $45.00 on December 23
New balance: _____

18. Old balance: $237.80

Check: #54 to The City Grill for $72.58 on March 3
Check: #55 to Home Finance Co. for $124.77 on March 3
Service charge: $6.40 on March 5
Deposit: $253.15 on March 8
Check: #56 to The Vision Place for $119.75 on March 10
Check: #57 to Pam's Fruit Stand for $25.39 on March 11
Deposit: $125.00 on March 12
New balance: _____

Name _____ Date _____

19. Old balance: $624.43

  Check: #234 to Brentwood Apartments for $415.50 on April 2

  Check: # 235 to Flower Mart for $18.50 on April 5

  Deposit: $321.84 on April 7

  Check: #237 to ABC Supermarket for $100 in April 14

  Check: #238 to Clark's Electronics for $176.45 on April 21

  New balance: _____

20. Old balance: $267.44

  Check: # 76 to Betty Beauty Supply for $19.50 on May 10

  Deposit: $365.79 on May 15

  Check: #77 to the Internet Provider for $53.76 on May 15

  Check: #78 to Dr. Selma Rubin for $60 on May 18

  Service charge: $7.50 on May 19

  Check: #79 to Enderton Electronics for $121.50 on May 22

  Deposit: $200 on May 28

  New balance: _____

Solve.

21. Alan had $342.09 in his checking account. He then wrote checks for $142.50, $53.80, and $29.85. What is the least amount he must transfer from his savings account in order to cover his car payment of $185.00? _____

22. Rosa began the month with a checking account balance of $74.30. She then deposited $275.88 and wrote checks for $113.70, $65.36, and $97.25. How much must she deposit in order to pay her rent of $295.00? _____

Name _____   Date _____

Reconciling a Checking Account Statement

When you have a checking account, your bank returns your **canceled checks** each month and sends you a computerized bank statement that includes a listing of your deposits and the amount paid by each check you have written. To check for any errors, it is important to reconcile your **check register** with the monthly bank statement.

Example: Your 12/10 bank statement shows your deposits and checks for the past month and shows an ending balance of $430.36. But, your check register shows a balance of $350.19 on that date. Reconcile this account statement given the facts that it shows a $7.25 service charge and that check #879 for $87.42 is still outstanding.

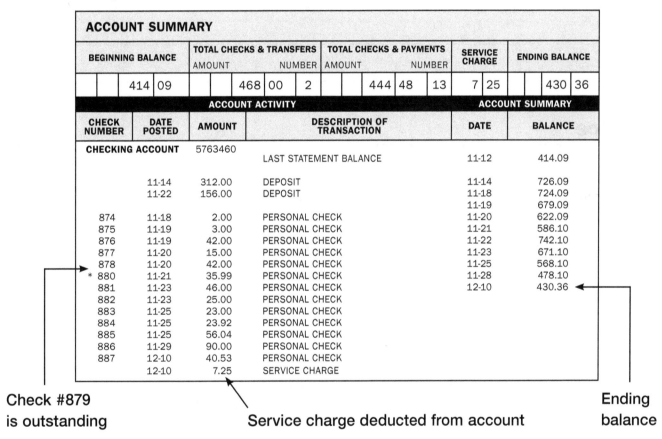

Check #879 is outstanding

Service charge deducted from account

Ending balance

THINK: The bank statement balance must be adjusted upward to account for outstanding deposits and downward to account for outstanding checks. Your register balance must be adjusted downward to account for the service charge.

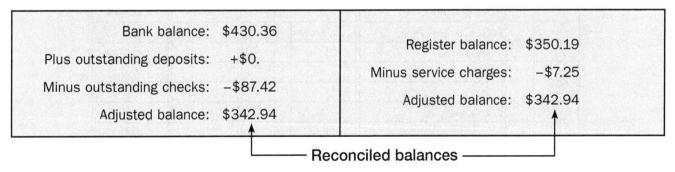

Reconciled balances

Name _____ Date _____

Think About It

1. Why is it important to save all of your canceled checks?

_____

_____

_____

2. Why do banks often charge customers a monthly service fee on a checking account?

_____

_____

_____

Practice

Remember to estimate whenever you use your calculator.

Use the bank statement and the check register below for Exercises 1–6.

CHECK NUMBER	DATE POSTED	AMOUNT	DESCRIPTION OF TRANSACTION	DATE	BALANCE
CHECKING ACCOUNT		5763460			
			LAST STATEMENT BALANCE	10-10	244.24
	10-24	312.00	DEPOSIT	10-24	555.24
683	10-27	18.00	PERSONAL CHECK	10-27	537.24
684	10-29	80.40	PERSONAL CHECK	10-29	436.84
* 686	11-12	38.00	PERSONAL CHECK	11-12	414.09
	11-12	4.75	SERVICE CHARGE		

		RECORD ALL CHARGES OR CREDITS THAT AFFECT YOUR ACCOUNT						
NUMBER	DATE	DESCRIPTION OF TRANSACTION	PAYMENT/DEBIT (−)	✔ T	FEE (IF ANY) (−)	DEPOSIT/ CREDIT (+)	\$ BALANCE 244	24
	10/24	Deposit	\$	\$		\$ 312.00	+ 312	00
							555	24
683	10/25	Norma's Yarn Shop	18.00				− 18	00
		sweater yarn					537	24
684	10/26	Southwestern Phone Co.	80.40				− 80	40
		phone bill					456	84
685	11/3	Worth's Catalog Sales	19.85				− 19	85
		jeans					436	99
686	11/10	Pat Simms, Inc.	38.00				− 38	00
							398	99

Name _____ Date _____

What is the:

1. Statement ending balance? _____

2. Check register balance? _____

3. Outstanding check number? _____

4. Amount of the outstanding check? _____

5. Service charge? _____

6. Actual reconciled statement balance? _____

Use the given information to reconcile the bank statement balance with the check register balance. Find the adjusted balance for each.

7. Check register balance: $479.70
   Statement ending balance: $582.43
   Outstanding checks: $76.40, $29.83
   Service charge: $3.50

   _____

8. Check register balance: $551.38
   Statement ending balance: $556.63
   Outstanding deposit: $75.00
   Outstanding checks: $62.45, $18.75
   Service charge: $0.95

   _____

9. Check register balance: $159.35
   Statement ending balance: $223.29
   Outstanding checks: $53.65, $14.79
   Service charge: $4.50

   _____

10. Check register balance: $254.15
    Statement ending balance: $295.01
    Outstanding checks: $28.95, $18.76
    Service charge: $6.85

    _____

11. Check register balance: $534.79
    Statement ending balance: $404.64
    Outstanding checks: $24.85
    Outstanding deposit: $150
    Service charge: $5.00

    _____

12. Check register balance: $477.32
    Statement ending balance: $495.76
    Outstanding checks: $45.95, $27.99
    Outstanding deposit: $50
    Service charge: $5.50

    _____

Name _____ Date _____

Use the bank statement and the check register below for Exercises 9–14. Remember to estimate whenever you use your calculator.

CHECK NUMBER	DATE POSTED	AMOUNT	DESCRIPTION OF TRANSACTION	DATE	BALANCE
CHECKING ACCOUNT		4583065	LAST STATEMENT BALANCE	6-06	389.68
	6-15	285.34	DEPOSIT	6-15	675.02
				6-19	619.13
475	6-19	55.89	PERSONAL CHECK	6-22	543.63
* 477	6-22	75.50	PERSONAL CHECK	7-03	526.68
478	7-03	16.95	PERSONAL CHECK	7-08	521.18
	7-08	5.50	SERVICE CHARGE		

RECORD ALL CHARGES OR CREDITS THAT AFFECT YOUR ACCOUNT

NUMBER	DATE	DESCRIPTION OF TRANSACTION	PAYMENT/DEBIT (−)	✔ T	FEE (IF ANY) (−)	DEPOSIT/ CREDIT (+)	BALANCE $ 389 68
	6/15	Deposit	$	$		$ 285.34	+ 285 34
							675 02
475	6/19	Clack's Clothing	55.89				− 55 89
		bathing suits					619 13
476	6/20	This Week Magazine	15.60				− 15 60
		Book					603 53
477	6/22	The Outdoors Shop	75.50				− 75 50
		Camping Things					528 03
478	7/3	Rebecca's Records	16.95				− 16 95
							511 08

What is the:

13. Statement ending balance? _____

14. Check register balance? _____

15. Outstanding check number? _____

16. Amount of the outstanding check? _____

17. Service charge? _____

18. Actual reconciled statement balance? _____

Problem Solving Application: Checking Accounts

If you have a checking account, it is important to keep an accurate record of your balance. The balance is the amount of money that is in the account.

Jane Caldwell Checkbook Record

Check Number	Date	Description of Transaction	Amount of Check	Amount of Deposit	Balance	
					250	00
101	11/6	Ted's Market	34.75		34	75
					215	25
	11/8	Deposit		95.87	95	87
					311	12

The checkbook record shows a beginning balance of $250.00.

On 11/6, Jane wrote a check for $34.75 to Ted's Market. The new balance was $215.25.

On 11/8, Jane deposited $95.87. The new balance was $311.12.

49

Name _____ Date _____

Find each new balance after the given transaction.

Check Number	Date	Description of Transaction	Amount of Check	Amount of Deposit	Balance	
					375	00
101	11/6	Deposit		50.85		
					1. _____	____
	11/8	John Forbes	55.25			
					2. _____	____
101	11/6	Book Mart	19.75			
					3. _____	____
101	11/6	Deposit		50.85		
					4. _____	____
	11/8	Pat Simms, Inc.	165.32			
					5. _____	____

Solve.

6. On 3/1, Sue opened a checking account with $425.00. On 3/8 she deposited $65.38 and wrote checks for $27.60 and $120.95. On 3/22, she deposited $75.32. What was Sue's new balance?

_____

Name _____   Date _____

Savings Accounts

You earn about $80.00 a week in a part-time job. You decide to open a **savings account** in order to save enough money for a down payment on a used car.

Example 1: You deposited $50.00 from your earnings plus a $25 check in your savings account. Review the **deposit slip** below and describe each of your entries.

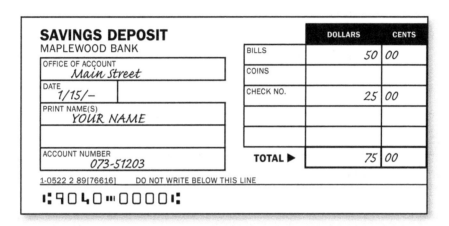

Example 2: After several months, you have saved over $900. You withdraw $650.00 to make the down payment on the used car. Review the **withdrawal slip** below and describe each of your entries.

Some savings account records are kept in a **passbook**. For these you need to bring your passbook to the bank each time you make a deposit or a withdrawal. The bank's computer enters each transaction in your passbook.

Example 3: You had a balance of $935.00 on June 2. You made a deposit of $62.50 on June 5, a withdrawal of $650.00 on June 11, another deposit of $52.00 on June 18, and had interest of $1.58 posted on July 1. What is your new savings account balance?

> **THINK:** Add deposits and interest. Subtract withdrawals.

Old Balance	+ Deposits	+ Interest	–Withdrawals	=New Balance
$935.00	+ $114.50	+ $1.58	–$650.00	= $401.08

Your new balance is $401.08. Review the savings account statement below.

Name	Your name			Account # 073-51203	
Date	**Deposit**	**Withdrawal**	**Interest**		**Balance**
6/2					$935.00
6/5	$62.50				$997.50
6/11		$650.00			$347.50
6/18	$52.00				$399.50
7/1			$1.58		$401.08

Name _____ Date _____

1. How are savings accounts different from checking accounts?

_____

_____

2. Why do banks pay interest on savings accounts?

_____

_____

Practice

Remember to estimate whenever you use your calculator.

Make up a deposit slip for the deposit. Use today's date and your own name. (Use the blank savings deposit slips on p. 135.)

1. $85.00 in cash and a check for $43.29

   Total deposit: _____

2. $32.00 in cash, $2.75 in coins, and checks for $134.80 and $32.53

   Total deposit: _____

3. Checks for $45.89, $187.40, and $14.50 and $25.00 in cash.

   Total deposit: _____

4. $10.50 in coins, $297.00 in cash, and checks for $135.00 and $273.65

   Total deposit: _____

5. $75.00 in cash and a check for $124.65

   Total deposit: _____

6. $27.00 in cash, $1.75 in coins, and checks for $215.50 and $89.34

   Total deposit: _____

7. Checks for $42.35, $55.89, and $74.40 and $21.50 and $54.80 in cash

   Total deposit: _____

8. $9.50 in coins, $370.00 in cash, and checks for $253.51 and $189.45

   Total deposit: _____

Name _____ Date _____

Copy the blank savings withdrawal slips from page 136. Make up a withdrawal slip for the withdrawal. Use today's date and your own name and signature.

9. $280.00

10. $437.88

11. $47.00

12. $1,350.65

Complete the table.

Old balance	Transaction	New balance
$143.78	Deposit: $44.79	13. _____
$76.95	Withdrawal: $35.00	14. _____
$388.39	Deposit: $128.73	15. _____
$37.51	Interest payment: $1.18	16. _____
$1,836.68	Deposit: $387.24	17. _____
$502.31	Withdrawal: $280.00	18. _____

Compute the running balances for this savings account.

Date	Deposit	Withdrawal	Interest	Balance
10/3				$73.98
10/5	$54.87			19. _____
10/9		$45.00		20. _____
10/12		$27.50		21. _____
10/19	$86.36			22. _____
10/20			$1.05	23. _____
10/27		$64.00		24. _____
10/30	$15.84			25. _____

The Mathematics of Banking and Credit, SV 9780547625614

Name _____ Date _____

Write the new balance for each transaction.

Old balance	Transaction	New balance
$123.85	Deposit: $50.89	26. _____
$84.23	Withdrawal: $25.00	27. _____
$427.56	Deposit: $245.12	28. _____
$53.27	Interest payment: $4.56	29. _____
$1,365.87	Withdrawal: $525.00	30. _____

Compute the running balances for this savings account.

Date	Deposit	Withdrawal	Interest	Balance
9/4				$65.34
9/5	$106.55			31. _____
9/10		$75.00		32. _____
9/13	$23.67			33. _____
9/22	$45.50			34. _____
9/27		$55.00		35. _____
9/28			$2.48	36. _____

The Mathematics of Banking and Credit, SV 9780547625614

Name _____ Date _____

Complete the table.

Old balance	Transaction	New balance
$95.06	Deposit: $20	37. _____
$216.28	Withdrawal: $50	38. _____
$487.35	Interest payment: $8.06	39. _____
$144.59	Deposit: $75.50	40. _____
$852.93	Withdrawal: $200.00	41. _____
$1,462.98	Deposit: $500.00	42. _____

Complete the running balances for this savings account.

Date	Deposit	Withdrawal	Interest	Balance
9/4				$450.82
9/5	$100.00			43. _____
9/10		$35.00		44. _____
9/13		$50.00		45. _____
9/22	$205.50			46. _____
9/27	$175.88			47. _____
9/28		$100.00		48. _____
9/28	$60.45			49. _____

The Mathematics of Banking and Credit, SV 9780547625614

Simple and Compound Interest

The **interest** you earn on your checking or savings accounts is determined by the interest **rate** expressed as an annual (yearly) percent, the **principal**, or amount of money in your account, and the length of **time** (in years) the money is used.

Simple interest is computed by using this formula.

Interest = Principal $\times$ Rate $\times$ Time, or $I = p \times r \times t$

Example 1: You deposit $400 in a savings account that pays 1.75% interest per year. How much interest will you earn in 3 months? How much will then be in your account?

THINK: Principal: $400   Rate: 1.75% = 0.0175   Time: 3 mo = $\frac{1}{4}$y = 0.25 y

Step 1	Multiply to find the interest earned.	$I = p \times r \times t$
		$I = \$400 \times 0.0175 \times 0.25$
		$I = \$1.75$

You will earn $1.75 in interest.

| **Step 2** | Add to find the new balance. | $\$400 + \$1.75 = \$401.75$ |

At the end of 3 months, you will have $401.75 in your account.

For longer periods of time, banks **compound** your interest. They periodically add the interest to your account and compute interest in successive periods on each new higher principal.

Example 2: Jeff deposits $800.00 in a savings account that pays 2% interest compounded quarterly. How much will be in the account at the end of 1 year? How much interest will he earn in 1 year?

THINK: Principal: $800   Rate: 2% = 0.02   Time: each $\frac{1}{4}$y = 0.25 y

| **Step 1** | Compute 1st-quarter interest and the new balance (principal). | $\$800.00 \times 0.02 \times 0.25 = \$4.00$ |
| | | $\$800.00 + \$4.00 = \$804.00$ |

| **Step 2** | Compute 2nd-quarter interest and the new balance (principal). | $\$804.00 \times 0.02 \times 0.25 = \$4.02$ |
| | | $\$804.00 + \$4.02 = \$808.02$ |

| **Step 3** | Compute 3rd-quarter interest and the new balance (principal). | $\$808.02 \times 0.02 \times 0.25 = \$4.04$ |
| | | $\$808.02 + \$4.04 = \$812.06$ |

| **Step 4** | Compute 4th-quarter interest and the new balance (principal). | $\$812.06 \times 0.02 \times 0.25 = \$4.06$ |
| | | $\$812.06 + \$4.06 = \$816.12$ |

At the end of 1 year, Jeff's new savings account balance will be $816.12.

| **Step 5** | Subtract to find the interest. | $\$816.12 - \$800.00 = \$16.12$ |

Jeff will earn $16.12 in interest.

Name _____ Date _____

Banks use a compound interest table to compute compound interest.

Example 3: Delia deposits $2,000 in a savings account that pays 2% interest compounded quarterly. How much will she have at the end of 3 years?

THINK: 4 quarters per year means 12 quarters in 3 years.
2% annual interest is equal to 0.5% interest per quarter.

| Step 1 | Use the table below to find the compounded value of $1.00

$1.00 at 0.5% for 12 periods will grow to $1.0617.

| Step 2 | Multiply to find the new balance (principal).
$2,000 × $1.0617 = $2,123.40

At the end of 3 years, Delia will have $2,123.40.

Compound Interest Table

No. of Periods	0.5%	1%	1.5%	2%	2.5%	3%	3.5%	4%
1	1.0050	1.0100	1.0150	1.0200	1.0250	1.0300	1.0350	1.0400
2	1.0100	1.0201	1.0302	1.0404	1.0506	1.0609	1.0712	1.0816
3	1.0151	1.0303	1.0457	1.0612	1.0769	1.0927	1.1087	1.1248
4	1.0202	1.0406	1.0614	1.0824	1.1038	1.1255	1.1475	1.1699
5	1.0253	1.0510	1.0773	1.1041	1.1314	1.1593	1.1877	1.2167
6	1.0304	1.0615	1.0934	1.1262	1.1597	1.1941	1.2293	1.2653
7	1.0355	1.0721	1.1098	1.1487	1.1887	1.2299	1.2723	1.3159
8	1.0407	1.0829	1.1265	1.1717	1.2184	1.2668	1.3168	1.3686
9	1.0459	1.0937	1.1434	1.1951	1.2489	1.3048	1.3629	1.4233
10	1.0511	1.1046	1.1605	1.2190	1.2801	1.3439	1.4106	1.4802
11	1.0564	1.1157	1.1779	1.2434	1.3121	1.3842	1.4600	1.5395
12	1.0617	1.1268	1.1956	1.2682	1.3449	1.4258	1.5111	1.6010
13	1.0670	1.1381	1.2136	1.2936	1.3785	1.4685	1.5640	1.6651
14	1.0723	1.1495	1.2318	1.3195	1.4130	1.5126	1.6187	1.7317
15	1.0777	1.1610	1.2502	1.3459	1.4483	1.5580	1.6753	1.8009
16	1.0831	1.1726	1.2690	1.3728	1.4845	1.6047	1.7340	1.8730
17	1.0885	1.1843	1.2880	1.4002	1.5216	1.6528	1.7947	1.9479
18	1.0939	1.1961	1.3073	1.4282	1.5597	1.7024	1.8575	2.0258
19	1.0994	1.2081	1.3270	1.4568	1.5987	1.7535	1.9225	2.1068
20	1.1049	1.2202	1.3469	1.4859	1.6386	1.8061	1.9898	2.1911
21	1.1104	1.2324	1.3671	1.5157	1.6796	1.8603	2.0594	2.2788
22	1.1160	1.2447	1.3876	1.5460	1.7216	1.9161	2.1315	2.3699
23	1.1216	1.2572	1.4084	1.5769	1.7646	1.9736	2.2061	2.4647
24	1.1272	1.2697	1.4295	1.6084	1.8087	2.0328	2.2833	2.5633
25	1.1328	1.2824	1.4509	1.6407	1.8539	2.0938	2.3673	2.6658

Name _____ Date _____

Think About It

1. Which earns more in a year, an account compounded quarterly or the same account compounded daily? Why?

   _____

   _____

   _____

2. Why do banks pay you less interest than they earn on your money?

   _____

   _____

   _____

Practice

Remember to estimate whenever you use your calculator.

Compute the simple interest earned and the new balance (principal).

Principal	Rate	Time	Interest; New Balance
$250	2%	4 y	1. _____ ; _____
$500	$1\frac{1}{2}$ %	3 y	2. _____ ; _____
$1,250	$2\frac{1}{2}$%	2 y	3. _____ ; _____
$8,020	3%	8 y	4. _____ ; _____
$3,500	$1\frac{1}{2}$ %	7 y	5. _____ ; _____
$850	$2\frac{1}{2}$%	10 y	6. _____ ; _____
$2,630	$2\frac{1}{4}$%	3 y	7. _____ ; _____
$5,875	$1\frac{3}{4}$%	5 y	8. _____ ; _____

Name _____ Date _____

Compute the new balance (principal) and the compound interest earned.

Principal	Rate	Time	Interest; New Balance
$1,000	2% compounded semiannually	1 y	**9.** _____ ; _____
$5,000	$1\frac{3}{4}$% compounded semiannually	2 y	**10.** _____ ; _____
$400	$2\frac{1}{2}$% compounded quarterly	1 y	**11.** _____ ; _____
$7,500	$1\frac{1}{2}$% compounded quarterly	18 mo	**12.** _____ ; _____

Use the compound interest table to find the new balance (principal).

Principal	Rate	Time	New Balance
$4,000	2% compounded annually	5 y	**13.** _____
$6,500	3% compounded semiannually	2 y	**14.** _____
$10,000	2% compounded quarterly	4 y	**15.** _____
$3,200	4% compounded quarterly	6 y	**16.** _____

The Mathematics of Banking and Credit, SV 9780547625614

Name _____ Date _____

| Extension | Money Market and NOW Accounts

Banks offer special checking accounts that allow you to earn interest. Most NOW and Money Market accounts require that you keep a minimum balance, such as $2,000 or $2,500. Interest is usually compounded daily and paid monthly on the basis of your average daily balance.

1. How do NOW and Money Market accounts differ from regular checking accounts?

_____

_____

2. If your $2\frac{1}{2}\%$ NOW account has an average daily balance of $2,500 over the course of a year, about how much interest would you earn? _____

Practice

Simple and Compound Interest

Compute the simple interest earned and the new balance (principal). Remember to estimate whenever you use your calculator.

Principal	Rate	Time	Simple Interest	New Balance
$350	6%	3 y	1. _____	2. _____
$600	5%	4 y	3. _____	4. _____
$1,250	7%	5 y	5. _____	6. _____
$4,050	6%	4 y	7. _____	8. _____
$6,550	8%	6 y	9. _____	10. _____
$2,550	$5\frac{1}{2}\%$	5 y	11. _____	12. _____
$950	$7\frac{1}{2}\%$	10 y	13. _____	14. _____

Name _____ Date _____

Compute the new balance (principal) and the compound interest earned.

Principal	Rate	Time	New Balance	Compound Interest
$2,000	6% compounded semiannually	1 y	15. _____	16. _____
$4,000	$5\frac{1}{4}$% compounded semiannually	2 y	17. _____	18. _____
$500	7% compounded quarterly	1 y	19. _____	20. _____
$6,500	$6\frac{1}{2}$% compounded quarterly	1 y	21. _____	22. _____
$3,500	$5\frac{3}{4}$% compounded quarterly	18 mo	23. _____	24. _____
$7,000	5% compounded semiannually	1 y	25. _____	27. _____

Use the compound interest table on page 58 to find the new balance (principal).

Principal	Rate	Time	New Balance
$5,000	8% compounded semiannually	4 y	27. _____
$4,500	6% compounded semiannually	5 y	28. _____
$12,000	7% compounded semiannually	7 y	29. _____
$3,300	10% compounded quarterly	6 y	30. _____
$10,000	8% compounded quarterly	5 y	31. _____
$8,500	6% compounded quarterly	4 y	32. _____

The Mathematics of Banking and Credit, SV 9780547625614

Problem Solving Application: Interest

A charge for the use of money is called interest. If you borrow money from a bank, you will need to pay interest for the use of the money. On the other hand, when you have money in a savings account, the bank pays interest for the use of your money.

One type of interest is called simple interest. To compute simple interest, use this formula:

Interest	=	Principal	×	Rate	×	Time
I	=	p	×	r	×	t

I is the amount of interest
p is the principal, which is the amount of money that is borrowed or is in the savings account
r is the *yearly* rate of interest
t is the time in years

How much interest do you have to pay if you borrow $500.00 for 6 months at a rate of 12% per year?

THINK: Principal = $500

rate = 12%, or 0.12

time = 6 mo = $\frac{6}{12}$ y, or $\frac{1}{2}$ y

$I = \$500 \times 0.12 \times \frac{1}{2}$

$I = \$60.00 \times \frac{1}{2}$

$I = \$30.00$

So, you would have to pay $30.00 in interest.

> **Think About It**

1. Some banks advertise their interest rates in newspapers. They offer free gifts to people who open accounts. Why should banks want additional money on which they will have to pay interest?

_____

_____

_____

Name _____ Date _____

Practice

Remember to estimate whenever you use your calculator.

Find the simple interest.

Interest	Principal	Rate	Time
1. _____	$1,000	6%	1 y
2. _____	$800	7%	2 y
3. _____	$1,200	9%	6 mo
4. _____	$2,000	10%	1 y 3 mo
5. _____	$5,000	$7\frac{1}{2}$%	18 mo
6. _____	$3,000	5%	2 y 4 mo
7. _____	$4,500	11%	9 mo
8. _____	$250	8%	3 mo
9. _____	$8,000	$6\frac{1}{4}$%	4 y
10. _____	$1,750	5.5%	1 y
11. _____	$10,000	12%	60 mo
12. _____	$9,800	11%	4 y 6 mo
13. _____	$500	15%	9 mo
14. _____	$5,000	15%	9 mo
15. _____	$50,000	15%	9 mo
16. _____	$500,000	15%	9 mo
17. _____	$12,800	$9\frac{3}{4}$%	3 y
18. _____	$975	$4\frac{1}{4}$%	3 mo
19. _____	$15,225	8.75%	16 mo
20. _____	$3,788	23%	90 d

The Mathematics of Banking and Credit, SV 9780547625614

Name _____ Date _____

Most banks pay **compound interest** on savings accounts. This means the interest is computed two or more times a year. If you do not withdraw your interest, it is credited to your account.

How much is the principal in your account after 6 months if you deposit $500 in a savings account that pays 4% interest compounded quarterly?

THINK: COMPOUNDED QUARTERLY MEANS FOUR TIMES A YEAR, OR EVERY 3 MONTHS.

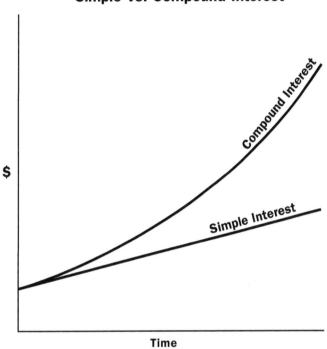

Simple Vs. Compound Interest

First quarter earnings

$I = \$500 \times 0.04 \times \frac{1}{4}$

$I = \$20 \times \frac{1}{4}$

$I = \$5.00$

So, the new principal is $500 + $5.00, or $505.00.

Second quarter earnings

$I = \$505.00 \times 0.04 \times \frac{1}{4}$

$I = \$20.20 \times \frac{1}{4}$

$I = \$5.05$

So, the new principal is $505.00 + $5.05, or $510.05.

The Mathematics of Banking and Credit, SV 9780547625614

Name _____ Date _____

Use the compound-interest information given on the previous page.
Find the amount of money in your account.

21. after 9 months.

_____

22. after 12 months.

_____

23. after 15 months.

_____

24. after 18 months.

_____

25. Find the principal after 1 year if $5,000 is deposited in a savings account that pays an annual interest rate of 3% compounded quarterly.

_____

26. How much interest will you earn in 9 months if you deposit $10,000 into a savings account that pays an annual interest rate of 4% compounded quarterly?

_____

Name _____ Date _____

Decision Making: Which Bank Account Is Best?

When you decide to open a checking account or a savings account, you are often confronted by many different types of accounts. You must examine the features of each and decide which is best for your own particular needs.

Problem A

Victoria has just started her first job and needs to open a checking account in order to deposit her weekly paychecks. So that Victoria can choose which type of account is best for her, the bank's customer service representative gave her a brochure describing the 4 types of checking accounts.

Regular Checking

Each month, your canceled checks are returned to you with a statement describing your account activity for the month. There is a $5.00 monthly service charge plus 25¢ per check.

NOW Checking

This account pays you 2% interest on your checking account balance which is compounded daily and paid monthly. Your NOW account is free if you keep the required minimum daily balance of $1,000 in your account. Below the minimum there is a $7.50 monthly service charge plus 25¢ per check.

Value Checking

This checking account is ideal for people who do not write many checks. There is no minimum balance and you can write up to 5 checks per month for free. If you write more than 5 checks, there is a monthly service charge of $6.00 plus 20¢ per check.

Money Market Checking

This account pays you about 3.5% on your checking account balance. Your money market account is free if you keep a minimum daily balance of $2,000 in your account. Below the minimum there is a $7.50 monthly service charge plus 25¢ per check.

www.harcourtschoolsupply.com
67
Part II
The Mathematics of Banking and Credit, SV 9780547625614

Name _____ Date _____

Decision-Making Factors

Compare the 4 options by completing the table.
- Minimum balance requirement
- Monthly service charge
- Cost per check
- Interest paid

Decision-Making Comparisons

Compare the 4 options by completing the table.

Factor	Regular	NOW	Value	Money Market
Minimum balance		1. _____	2. _____	3. _____
Monthly service charge (if conditions not met)	4. _____	5. _____	$6.00	6. _____
Cost per check (if conditions not met)	7. _____	25¢	8. _____	9. _____
Interest paid	10. _____	11. _____	12. _____	Yes, about 3.5%

Making the Decisions

Which account should Victoria open:

13. If the amount of interest earned were the only factor?

_____

14. If she expects to write about 10 checks per month and does not expect to have more than about $1,000 in her account?

_____

15. If she expects to maintain a low balance and to write only 3 or 4 checks per month?

_____

16. If she has no problem maintaining a minimum balance of $1,000?

_____

17. What is the monthly service charge if she opens a Regular checking account and writes 12 checks per month?

_____

How much is this per year?

_____

18. What is the monthly service charge if she opens a NOW account and writes 12 checks per month and maintains a minimum balance of $1,000?

_____

19. What is the monthly service charge on a NOW account if she writes 15 checks per month and does not maintain a minimum balance of $1,000?

_____

20. Suppose Victoria can earn an average of $5.00 interest per month on a Money Market account and can maintain a minimum balance of $2,000. What would be her net annual savings over the Regular account in Question 17?

_____

21. Do you think that the free checking accounts are worth the minimum balance requirements and the higher service charge penalties?

_____

22. Which account would you choose? Why?

_____

Problem B

After Victoria has worked for several months, her checking account balance has been consistently high enough that she decides to open a savings account. She gets information on the types of savings accounts available so that she can choose which one is best for her.

Regular Savings	Money Market Savings
• *Can be opened with as little as $5*	• *Can be opened with $1,500 or more*
• *Unlimited deposits and withdrawals*	• *Limit of 5 withdrawals per month*
• *$1\frac{1}{2}$% interest*	• *Variable interest from 2% up, adjusted weekly*
• *No service charge*	• *$3.00 per month service charge if balance falls below $1,500*

Decision-Making Factors

• Initial deposit	• Access to money
• Interest rate	• Service charge

Name _____   Date _____

Decision-Making Comparisons

Compare the 2 options by completing the table.

Factor	Regular savings	Money Market savings
Initial deposit	23. _____	24. _____
Access to money	Any day	25. _____
Interest rate	26. _____	Variable
Service charge	27. _____	28. _____

Making the Decisions

Which account should Victoria open:

29. If she only has a small amount of money?

_____

30. If she wants to earn the most interest and she does have $3,000 to deposit?

_____

31. If she expects to make frequent deposits and withdrawals?

_____

32. If she would like to earn 3% interest?

_____

33. If the Money Market savings account averaged $2\frac{1}{2}$% interest, how much more could Victoria earn per year over a Regular savings account on a $10,000 deposit?

_____

34. Which account would you open? Why?

_____

Name _____ Date _____

Decision Making: More Practice

Dan is going to choose from among these 4 types of checking accounts.

Regular Checking

Each month, your cancelled checks are returned to you with a statement that describes your account activity for the month. There is a $6.50 monthly service charge plus 20¢ per check.

Value Checking

In this checking account, you can write up to 6 checks per month free. If you write more than 6 checks, there is a monthly service charge of $7.00 plus 20¢ per check.

NOW Checking

This account earns $5\frac{1}{2}\%$ interest on the checking account balance, compounded daily and paid monthly. The account is free if you keep the required minimum daily balance of $1,500. Below the minimum there is a $6.50 monthly service charge plus 20¢ per check.

Money Market Checking

This account pays you about 8% on your checking account balance. The account is free if you keep a minimum daily balance of $2,500 in your account. Below the minimum there is a $6.50 monthly service charge plus 25¢ per check.

Compare the 4 options by completing the table.

Factor	Regular	NOW	Value	Money Market
Minimum balance	1. _____	None	2. _____	3. _____
Monthly service charge (if conditions not met)	$6.50	4. _____	5. _____	6. _____
Cost per check (if conditions not met)	7. _____	8. _____	20¢	9. _____
Interest paid	10. _____	11. _____	12. _____	About 8%

Name _____ Date _____

Which account should Dan open:

13. If he has no problem maintaining a minimum balance of $1,500?

_____

14. If the amount of interest earned were the only factor?

_____

15. What is the monthly service charge if he opens a NOW account and writes 15 checks per month and maintains a minimum balance of $1,500?

_____

16. What is the monthly service charge on a NOW account if he writes 12 checks per month and does not maintain a minimum balance of $1,500?

_____

17. What is the monthly service charge if he opens a Regular checking account and writes 8 checks per month? How much is this per year?

_____

18. Suppose Dan earns an average of $6.00 interest per month on a Money Market account and maintains a minimum balance of $2,500. What would be his net annual savings over the Regular account in question 17?

_____

The Mathematics of Banking and Credit, SV 9780547625614

Money Tips 1

You can save time at the bank by using ATMs (Automated Teller Machines) and save money on transaction fees if the ATMs are owned by the bank. Furthermore, if your bank offers an **online banking** option, you can avoid fees and save time by using a home computer to do your banking.

Let's Look At The Facts

Banks have ATMs, which allow customers to use a special bank card to conduct certain transactions, even if the bank itself is closed. Some of these banks do not own their ATMs and may charge $1.00 or more for every transaction. With bank-owned ATMs, there is either a much lower transaction fee or no fee at all.

Banks that have secure websites that allow online banking sometimes offer free or reduced service charges to their customers who bank online instead of visiting the bank.

Let's Discuss Why

1. For what types of transactions might an ATM be used?

_____

_____

2. For what types of transactions might online banking be used instead of an ATM?

_____

_____

3. What are the advantages of dealing with a bank that has ATMs and online banking?

_____

_____

4. Why do you think banks that do not own their ATMs charge higher transaction fees?

_____

5. More banks charge an ATM transaction fee for withdrawals than for deposits. What might be the reason for this?

_____

_____

6. If the ABC Bank charges $1.00 per transaction and you use its ATMs 12 times per month, how much would you pay per year for this service?

_____

_____

7. If you use the XYZ Bank's ATMs and pay only 20¢ per transaction, how much would you save in a year over what you would pay to use the ABC Bank's ATMs in Exercise 6?

_____

_____

8. How could you find out if you are paying ATM transaction fees?

_____

_____

Let's See What You Would Do

9. Last year, it cost you $90 (75¢ per transaction) to use ATMs at the Capital City Bank, which has 16 locations around the city. The Warshaw County Bank charges no fee but has only 2 ATM locations, one near your office and one at the airport. Discuss the pros and cons of switching your accounts to the Warshaw Bank.

_____

_____

_____

10. The Olympia Federal Bank issues you a special bank card and assigns you a **Personal Identification Number (PIN)** so you can use its ATMs. This is your number exclusively and must be entered into an ATM before any transaction can be conducted. Why should you never give your PIN to someone else?

_____

_____

Calculator: Fractions on a Calculator

You have learned that you can rename fractions and mixed numbers as decimals by dividing the numerator by the denominator. You can also use a calculator to rename a fraction or mixed number as a decimal.

Rename $2\frac{4}{5}$ as a decimal.

Procedure	**Calculator Entry**	**Calculator Display**
Step 1 Divide the numerator of the fraction by the denominator.	$\boxed{4}$ $\boxed{\div}$ $\boxed{5}$ $\boxed{=}$	0.8
Step 2 Add the whole number.	$\boxed{+}$ $\boxed{2}$ $\boxed{=}$	2.8

So $2\frac{4}{5} = 2.8$.

To rename a fraction or a mixed number as a percent, first use the calculator to rename it as a decimal. Then multiply by 100.

Rename $\frac{3}{8}$ as a decimal.

Procedure	**Calculator Entry**	**Calculator Display**
Step 1 Divide the numerator by the denominator.	$\boxed{3}$ $\boxed{\div}$ $\boxed{8}$ $\boxed{=}$	0.375
Step 2 Multiply by 100.	$\boxed{\times}$ $\boxed{1}$ $\boxed{0}$ $\boxed{0}$ $\boxed{=}$	37.5

So $\frac{3}{8} = 37.5\%$.

Name _____ Date _____

Use a calculator to rename the fraction or mixed number as a decimal. When necessary, round your answer to the nearest thousandth.

1. $\frac{5}{8}$ _____

2. $\frac{7}{20}$ _____

3. $\frac{3}{7}$ _____

4. $4\frac{3}{5}$ _____

5. $6\frac{1}{6}$ _____

6. $\frac{3}{4}$ _____

Use a calculator to rename the fraction or mixed number as a percent. When necessary, round your answer to the nearest tenth of a percent.

7. $\frac{9}{20}$ _____

8. $\frac{11}{25}$ _____

9. $\frac{5}{7}$ _____

10. $\frac{1}{6}$ _____

11. $3\frac{3}{5}$ _____

12. $9\frac{12}{25}$ _____

13. $6\frac{9}{16}$ _____

14. $7\frac{5}{6}$ _____

15. $8\frac{1}{3}$ _____

16. If your calculator has a percent key, [%], describe how to rename $\frac{3}{8}$ as a percent.

_____

The Mathematics of Banking and Credit, SV 9780547625614

Part II Review

Vocabulary

Choose the letter of the word(s) that completes the sentence.

1. Money placed by you into a savings or a checking account is called _____.

   a. A withdrawal   **b.** A deposit   **c.** Interest

2. Money that is added to your account by the bank is called _____.

   a. A withdrawal   **b.** A deposit   **c.** Interest

3. When interest is compounded quarterly, it is paid to you _____ times per year..

   a. One   **b.** Two   **c.** Four

Skills

Find the new bank account balance.

4. Old balance: $387.87
   Check: $37.75
   Deposit: $123.30
   Check: $23.08
   Check: $76.57

   _____

5. Old balance: $1,835. 94
   Check: $274.33
   Check: $88.27
   Service charge: $3.50
   Deposit: $385.89

   _____

6. Old balance: $500.00
   Withdrawal: $175.00
   Withdrawal: $60.00
   Deposit: $37.50

   _____

7. Old balance: $675.30
   Deposit: $50
   Interest: $1.13
   Withdrawal: $185.00

   _____

Name _____   Date _____

Use the given information to reconcile the bank statement balance with the check register balance. Find the adjusted balance for each.

8. Check register balance: $217.84

   Statement ending balance: $279.50

   Outstanding checks: $15.80, $49.71

   Service charge: $3.85

   _____

9. Check register balance: $87.50

   Statement ending balance: $137.90

   Outstanding check: $75.00

   Outstanding deposit: $19.85

   Service charge: $4.75

   _____

Find the answer.

10. How much simple interest will be earned in 3 years on $2,500 in an account that pays 1.5%?

    _____

11. What will be the new balance on $800 in an account that earns 2% simple interest for 5 years?

    _____

12. Use the compound interest table on page 58. How much interest will be paid on $400 earning 2% compounded quarterly after 4 years?

    _____

13. Use the compound interest table on page 58. What will be the new balance on $5,000 earning 3% compounded semiannually after 10 years?

    _____

Name _____ Date _____

Part II Test

Make up a check for the payment. Use today's date and your own name and signature.

YOUR NAME	_____ DATE	**136**
		51-57/119
PAY TO THE ORDER OF _____		\$
_____ DOLLARS		
MAPPLEWOOD BANK		
MEMO _____	_____	
⑈011900671⑈ 976346 0⑉ 0880		

1. Check #136 to Dr. Robin Yeats for $65.00

2. Check #137 to Security Insurance Co. for $258.34

3. Check #264 to News Delivery Inc. for $12.50

4. Check #353 to Dr. Alexander Hart for $50.00

Make up a deposit slip for the deposit. Use the sample provided.

5. A check for $180 and a check for $18.75

   Total deposit: _____

6. A check for $77.50 and a check for $75 in cash

   Total deposit: _____

SAVINGS DEPOSIT MAPLEWOOD BANK			DOLLARS	CENTS
OFFICE OF ACCOUNT		BILLS	COINS	COINS
		COINS	CHECK NO.	CHECK NO.
DATE		CHECK NO.		
PRINT NAME(S)				
ACCOUNT NUMBER		TOTAL ▶		
1-0522 2 89[76616] DO NOT WRITE BELOW THIS LINE				
⑈9040⑉0000⑈				

Find the new account balance.

7. Old balance: $783.21

   Check: $73.90

   Check: $182.70

   Check: $57.24

   Service charge: $8.30

   _____

8. Old balance: $1,284.89

   Deposit: $231.48

   Check: $83.90

   Check: $374.50

   Check: $214.38

   _____

Use the given information to reconcile the bank statement balance with the check register balance. Find the adjusted balance for each.

9. Check register balance: $86.30

   Statement ending balance: $171.54

   Outstanding checks: $3.90, $87.74

   Service charge: $6.40

   _____

10. Check register balance: $486.35

    Statement ending balance: $500.75

    Outstanding checks: $29.40, $165.00

    Outstanding deposit: $176.50

    Service charge: $3.50

    _____

The Mathematics of Banking and Credit, SV 9780547625614

Solve.

11. Martha had $378.18 in her checking account. She then wrote checks for $125.87, $36.50, and $16.85. What is the least amount she must deposit in order to cover her rent of $345.50?

_____

12. Greg began the month with a balance of $68.14 in his checking account. He deposited $425.50 and wrote checks for $176.49 and $205.33. How much must he deposit in order to cover his truck payment of $185.35?

_____

13. Jim opened a savings account with a deposit of $250.00. He later deposited $45.00 and then withdrew $120. The bank posted interest of $1.56. What is his new balance?

_____

14. Sarah's savings account balance was $218.00. She withdrew $50 one month and deposited $40 the next. She then withdrew $75. The bank posted interest of $2.15. What is her new balance?

_____

Find the simple interest.

15. $600 at 1.5% for 10 years _____

16. $2,300 at $2\frac{1}{2}$ % for 4 years_____

Use the compound interest table on page 58 to find the new balance.

17. $2,500 at 2% compounded semiannually for 4 years

_____

18. $6,000 at 2% compounded quarterly for 5 years

_____

Part III:
Credit

Pre-Skills Test

Round to the nearest cent.

1. $27.868 _____
2. $4.923 _____
3. $30.905 _____

4. $86.2073 _____
5. $0.0753 _____
6. $0.0523 _____

Rename as a decimal.

7. 15% _____
8. 53% _____
9. 7% _____

10. 3% _____
11. 105% _____
12. 156% _____

Rename as a decimal.

13. 1% _____
14. 1.5% _____
15. $1\frac{1}{4}$% _____

16. 0.0405% _____
17. 0.06308% _____
18. 0.05506% _____

Multiply.

19. $0.9 \times \$40 =$ _____
20. $0.8 \times \$35 =$ _____

21. $0.7 \times \$78 =$ _____
22. $0.6 \times \$835 =$ _____

23. $0.35 \times \$700 =$ _____
24. $0.46 \times \$950 =$ _____

25. $0.79 \times \$748 =$ _____
26. $0.86 \times \$739 =$ _____

Name _____ Date _____

Multiply. Round to the nearest cent.

27. $6 \times \$5.128 = $ _____

28. $4 \times \$3.752 = $ _____

29. $40 \times \$1.499 = $ _____

30. $0.73 \times \$678.20 = $ _____

31. $0.43 \times \$809.49 = $ _____

32. $0.74 \times \$287.51 = $ _____

33. $0.67 \times \$526.43 = $ _____

34. $0.83 \times \$1,012.56 = $ _____

35. $0.015 \times \$2,023.63 = $ _____

36. $0.075 \times \$59.50 = $ _____

37. $0.0013 \times \$319.26 = $ _____

38. $0.00046 \times \$607.43 = $ _____

Find the answer to the nearest cent.

39. What is 13% of $528.20? _____

40. What is 17% of $832.78? _____

41. What is 18.6% of $409.86? _____

42. What is 19.65% of $689.53? _____

43. What is $1\frac{1}{2}$% of $25.50? _____

44. What is 1.3% of $62.82? _____

45. What is 0.04657% of $33? _____

46. What is 0.02342% of $18.75? _____

Using Credit Cards

Only you can decide whether or not you should get a **credit card**. Once you get a card, you must accept the responsibility for using it.

You used your credit card to charge a sweater at The Clothing Mart. The sweater cost $34.97. In the store, you looked over the **charge receipt** to make sure that all the entries were correct.

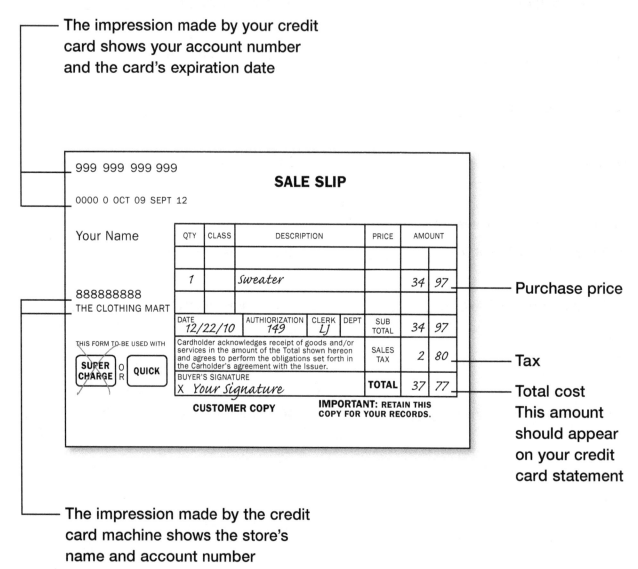

The impression made by your credit card shows your account number and the card's expiration date

SALE SLIP

999 999 999 999

0000 0 OCT 09 SEPT 12

Your Name

888888888
THE CLOTHING MART

THIS FORM TO-BE USED WITH

SUPER CHARGE O R QUICK

QTY	CLASS	DESCRIPTION	PRICE	AMOUNT	
1		Sweater		34	97

| DATE 12/22/10 | AUTHIORIZATION 149 | CLERK LJ | DEPT | SUB TOTAL | 34 | 97 |

Cardholder acknowledges receipt of goods and/or services in the amount of the Total shown hereon and agrees to perform the obligations set forth in the Carholder's agreement with the Issuer.

| SALES TAX | 2 | 80 |

BUYER'S SIGNATURE
X Your Signature

| TOTAL | 37 | 77 |

CUSTOMER COPY   **IMPORTANT: RETAIN THIS COPY FOR YOUR RECORDS.**

— Purchase price

— Tax

— Total cost
This amount should appear on your credit card statement

The impression made by the credit card machine shows the store's name and account number

Example 1: Identify the parts of the charge receipt.

At the end of the month, you got a statement that showed your charges, payments, the amount you owe, and other important information. You compared the amount with your charge receipts.

Name _____ Date _____

Example 2: Identify the parts of the monthly **credit card statement**.

Statement closing date

Your account number.

Charges and payments made by this date are included on this statement.

The amount you can charge without making a payment.

Charges and payments made this month. Check these against your records.

The Annual Percentage Rate (APR) is the interest you pay.

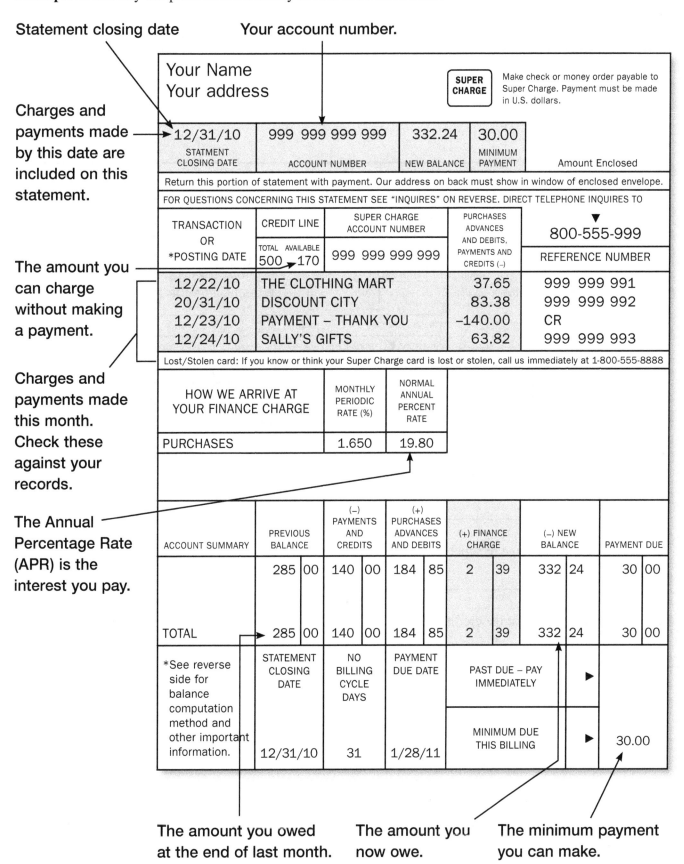

Your Name
Your address

SUPER CHARGE

Make check or money order payable to Super Charge. Payment must be made in U.S. dollars.

12/31/10	999 999 999 999	332.24	30.00	
STATEMENT CLOSING DATE	ACCOUNT NUMBER	NEW BALANCE	MINIMUM PAYMENT	Amount Enclosed

Return this portion of statement with payment. Our address on back must show in window of enclosed envelope.

FOR QUESTIONS CONCERNING THIS STATEMENT SEE "INQUIRES" ON REVERSE. DIRECT TELEPHONE INQUIRES TO

TRANSACTION OR *POSTING DATE	CREDIT LINE	SUPER CHARGE ACCOUNT NUMBER	PURCHASES ADVANCES AND DEBITS, PAYMENTS AND CREDITS (–)	▼ 800-555-999
	TOTAL AVAILABLE 500 → 170	999 999 999 999		REFERENCE NUMBER
12/22/10	THE CLOTHING MART		37.65	999 999 991
20/31/10	DISCOUNT CITY		83.38	999 999 992
12/23/10	PAYMENT – THANK YOU		–140.00	CR
12/24/10	SALLY'S GIFTS		63.82	999 999 993

Lost/Stolen card: If you know or think your Super Charge card is lost or stolen, call us immediately at 1-800-555-8888

HOW WE ARRIVE AT YOUR FINANCE CHARGE	MONTHLY PERIODIC RATE (%)	NORMAL ANNUAL PERCENT RATE	
PURCHASES	1.650	19.80	

ACCOUNT SUMMARY	PREVIOUS BALANCE	(–) PAYMENTS AND CREDITS	(+) PURCHASES ADVANCES AND DEBITS	(+) FINANCE CHARGE	(–) NEW BALANCE	PAYMENT DUE
	285 00	140 00	184 85	2 39	332 24	30 00
TOTAL	285 00	140 00	184 85	2 39	332 24	30 00

*See reverse side for balance computation method and other important information.	STATEMENT CLOSING DATE	NO BILLING CYCLE DAYS	PAYMENT DUE DATE	PAST DUE – PAY IMMEDIATELY	►	
				MINIMUM DUE THIS BILLING	►	30.00
	12/31/10	31	1/28/11			

The amount you owed at the end of last month.

The amount you now owe.

The minimum payment you can make.

The Mathematics of Banking and Credit, SV 9780547625614

Name _____ Date _____

1. How would you check your credit card receipts against a credit card statement?

_____

_____

Practice

Remember to estimate whenever you use your calculator.

You also have a credit card to buy gasoline. Look at the charge receipt.

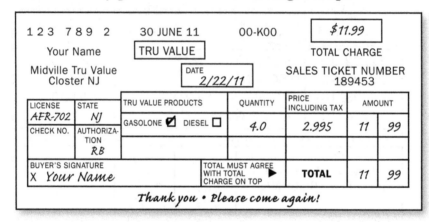

1 2 3 7 8 9 2	30 JUNE 11	00-K00	$11.99

Your Name   TRU VALUE   TOTAL CHARGE

Midville Tru Value
Closter NJ   DATE
2/22/11   SALES TICKET NUMBER
189453

LICENSE	STATE	TRU VALUE PRODUCTS	QUANTITY	PRICE INCLUDING TAX	AMOUNT	
AFR-702	NJ	GASOLONE ☑ DIESEL ☐	4.0	2.995	11	99
CHECK NO.	AUTHORIZA-TION RB					
BUYER'S SIGNATURE X Your Name		TOTAL MUST AGREE WITH TOTAL CHARGE ON TOP ▶	**TOTAL**		11	99

Thank you • Please come again!

What is:

1. Your credit card account number?

_____

2. The date of this charge receipt?

_____

3. The expiration date of the credit card?

_____

4. The total amount of this charge?

_____

5. The cost of a gallon of gasoline?

_____

6. The license plate number of the car that got the gasoline?

_____

Name _____ Date _____

Look at the gasoline credit card statement below.

TRU VALUE		123 789 456 2 **CREDIT CARD NUMBER**					**MINIMUM PAYMENT** 75.00		**NEW BALANCE** 142.93	

FEB. 28, 2011
STATEMENT CLOSING DATE   Your name
                                            Your address

TRANSACTION DATE		SALE TICKET NUMBER	CARD NUMBER			TRANSACTION DESCRIPTION & PURCHASE LOCATION *(See Reverse Side For Description of Codes)*			AMOUNT
1	03	4368221	001	01	210	KINOAKMCK	WESTWOOD	NJ	10.85
1	12	1527363	001	01	881	PIERMONT	CLOSTER	NJ	9.60
2	19					PAYMENT –			79.39CR
2	20	1523642	001	01	681	PIERMONT	CLOSTER	NJ	9.00
2	22	1196543	001	01	1	MIOVALE	CLOSTER	NJ	10.50
2	22	1894583	001	01	1	MIOVALE	CLOSTER	NJ	11.10
2	23	4365454	001	01	210	KINOAKMCK	WESTWOOD	NJ	11.00

Previous Balance	Payments & Credits		Purchase & Adjustments	FINANCE CHARGES		New Balance
158.88	−	79.39	+	+ 1.39	=	142.93

FINANCE CHARGE INFORMATION			Statement Closing Date	Credit Card Number	Minimum Payment
	PERIODIC RATE	ANNUAL PERCENTAGE RATE	FEB 28 11	123 789 456 2	75.00
To $ 500	1.75%	21%	To Avoid Additional FINANCE CHARGE New Balance Must be Recieved By MAR 20 11		**TRU VALUE**
Over $ 500	1.5%	18%			

What is:

7. The statement closing date? _____

8. Your credit card account number? _____

9. The previous balance? _____

10. Last month's payment? _____

11. The purchase total? _____

12. The finance charge? _____

13. The new balance? _____

14. The minimum payment? _____

15. What is the Annual Percentage Rate (APR) finance charge for amounts up to $500?

_____

16. What is the Annual Percentage Rate (APR) finance charge for amounts over $500?

_____

17. How much was charged on 2/20?

_____

18. How much was charged in January?

_____

Credit Finance Charges

On your credit card statement, the **finance charge** is the amount you pay if the last balance has not been paid in full. The **unpaid balance** is any of the last balance that was not paid. The **new balance** is the amount you now owe.

New Balance = Unpaid Balance + Finance Charge + New Charges

Example 1: Last month's balance was $285.00, of which $140.00 has been paid. Your new charges this month totaled $184.85. Your credit card company charges you 1.65% of the unpaid balance as a finance charge. Find the unpaid balance, the finance charge, and the new balance.

| **Step 1** | Subtract to find the unpaid balance. | $285 − $140 = $145 |
| | The unpaid balance is $145. | |

Step 2	Multiply to find the finance charge.	
	THINK: 1.65% = 0.0165	0.0165 × $145 = $2.3925
	The finance charge is $2.39.	

| **Step 3** | Add to find the new balance. | $145 + $2.39 + $184.85 = $332.24 |
| | The new balance is $332.24. | |

Some credit cards have variable finance rates as shown below.

$1\frac{1}{2}\%$ on the first $500 of unpaid balance   1% on the unpaid balance above $500

Example 2: The unpaid balance on Myra's account was $1,250. There were no new charges this month. Find the finance charge and the new balance.

| **Step 1** | Multiply to find the finance charge on the first $500. | |
| | **THINK:** $1\frac{1}{2}\%$ = 0.015 | 0.015 × $500 = $7.50 |

| **Step 2** | Multiply to find the finance charge on the amount over $500. | |
| | **THINK:** $1,250 − $500 = $750 and 1% = 0.01 | 0.01 × $750 = $7.50 |

| **Step 3** | Add to find the total finance charge. | $7.50 + $7.50 = $15.00 |
| | The total finance charge is $15.00 | |

| **Step 4** | Add to find the new balance. | $1,250 + $15.00 = $1,265 |
| | The new balance is $1,265. | |

Name _____ Date _____

1. What are some of the advantages and disadvantages of having a credit card?

_____

_____

_____

_____

Practice

Remember to estimate whenever you use your calculator.
Find the unpaid balance, the finance charge, and the new balance to the nearest cent.

1. Last balance: $80.45
Payments: $0
Finance rate: 1%
New charges: $99.85

Unpaid balance: _____

Finance charge: _____

New balance: _____

2. Last balance: $40.55
Payments: $0
Finance rate: 1.3%
New charges: $88.75

Unpaid balance: _____

Finance charge: _____

New balance: _____

3. Last balance: $143.50
Payments: $100.00
Finance rate: 1%
New charges: $0

Unpaid balance: _____

Finance charge: _____

New balance: _____

4. Last balance: $89.77
Payments: $19.00
Finance rate: 1.5%
New charges: $0
Unpaid balance: _____

Finance charge: _____

New balance: _____

5. Last balance: $530.85
Payments: $125.00
Finance rate: 1.2%
New charges: $0
Unpaid balance: _____

Finance charge: _____

New balance: _____

6. Last balance: $509.65
Payments: $350.00
Finance rate: $1\frac{1}{4}$%
New charges: $199.89
Unpaid balance: _____

Finance charge: _____

New balance: _____

7. Last balance: $90.85
Payments: $55.00
Finance rate: $1\frac{1}{2}$%
New charges: $345.90
Unpaid balance: _____

Finance charge: _____

New balance: _____

8. Last balance: $1,025.63
Payments: $750.00
Finance rate: $\frac{3}{4}$%
New charges: $836.25
Unpaid balance: _____

Finance charge: _____

New balance: _____

9. Last balance: $261.65
Payments: $43.30
Finance rate: 1.5%
New charges: $35.49
Unpaid balance: _____

Finance charge: _____

New balance: _____

Name _____ Date _____

Use the variable rates in Example 2 on page 88. Find the total finance charge on the given unpaid balance to the nearest cent.

10. $545.00 _____

11. $718.00 _____

12. $1,465 _____

13. $678.52 _____

14. $2,045.67 _____

Use the variable rates in Example 2. Find the unpaid balance, the finance charge, and the new balance to the nearest cent.

Last balance	Payments	New Charges	Unpaid Balance	Finance Charge	New Balance
$234.00	$0	$345.00	15. _____;	_____;	_____
$1,089.00	$500.00	$0	16. _____;	_____;	_____
$2,534.58	$750.58	$234.00	17. _____;	_____;	_____
$345.68	$35.89	$38.34	18. _____;	_____;	_____

Extension   **Minimum Payments**

Some credit card companies require a minimum payment on the new balance. Your new balance is $250. The minimum payment is 15% of the new balance. What is the minimum payment?

Multiply the new balance by 0.15. $0.15 \times \$250 = \$37.50$ minimum payment

Find the minimum payment.

1. The minimum payment is 12% of the new balance. The new balance is $456. _____

2. The minimum payment is 15% of the new balance or $25, whichever is greater.

   The new balance is $158. _____

Practice

Credit Finance Charges

Find the unpaid balance, the finance charge, and the new balance. Round each amount to the nearest cent. Remember to estimate whenever you use your calculator.

1. Last balance: $105.20
   Payments: $0
   Finance rate: $1\frac{1}{4}\%$
   New charges: $42.06

   Unpaid balance: _____

   Finance charge: _____

   New balance: _____

2. Last balance: $96.80
   Payments: $0
   Finance rate: $1\frac{1}{2}\%$
   New charges: $113.40

   Unpaid balance: _____

   Finance charge: _____

   New balance: _____

3. Last balance: $72.89
   Payments: $0
   Finance rate: 1.4%
   New charges: $36.99

   Unpaid balance: _____

   Finance charge: _____

   New balance: _____

4. Last balance: $198.60
   Payments: $65.40
   Finance rate: 1.2%
   New charges: $0

   Unpaid balance: _____

   Finance charge: _____

   New balance: _____

5. Last balance: $902.03
   Payments: $780.00
   Finance rate: $1\frac{3}{4}\%$
   New charges: $211.45

   Unpaid balance: _____

   Finance charge: _____

   New balance: _____

6. Last balance: $399.38
   Payments: $27.50
   Finance rate: 1.2%
   New charges: $514.80

   Unpaid balance: _____

   Finance charge: _____

   New balance: _____

Use the following variable rates to find the total finance charge on the given unpaid balance. Round each amount to the nearest cent.

Variable Rates: 1.25% on the first $500 of the unpaid balance
              0.75% on the unpaid balance above $500

7. $389.60 _____

8. $998.45 _____

9. $1,604.08 _____

10. $729.61 _____

11. $3,462.48 _____

91

Overdraft Checking

The bank agreed to lend you up to $500 to cover overdrafts. An overdraft is a check written for more than the balance in your account.

Interest = Daily Interest Rate × Sum of the Daily Balances

Example 1: The sum of your daily balances for the month was $2,700.
The **Annual Percentage Rate (APR)** is 17%. How much interest will you pay?

THINK: Look across from 17% to find the daily interest rate of 0.04657%.

Multiply to find the interest.
THINK: 0.04657% = 0.0004657

0.0004657 × $2,700 = $1.25739

You will pay $1.26 in interest.

Annual percentage rate	Daily interest rate
20%	0.05479%
19%	0.05205%
18%	0.04931%
17%	0.04657%

You can calculate the sum of the daily balances.

Example 2: On February 1, the balance in your overdraft account was $245.80.
On February 16, you wrote a $212.50 check. New balance: $458.30.
On February 23, you made a $50 payment. New balance: $408.30
The APR is 19%. Find the interest and the new balance.

Step 1 Find the sum of the daily balances for February.

Dates	Balance		Number of days	Sum of the balances
Feb. 1–15	$245.80	×	15	= $3,687.00
Feb. 16–22	$458.30	×	7	= $3,208.10
Feb. 23–28	$408.30	×	6	= $2,449.80
Total:			28	$9,344.90

| Step 2 | Find the daily interest rate for an APR of 19%.   0.05205% |

| Step 3 | Multiply to find the interest. |

THINK: 0.05205% = 0.0005205 $0.0005205 \times \$9,344.90 = \$4.8640204$

The interest is $4.86.

| Step 4 | Add to find the new balance. $\$408.30 + \$4.86 = \$413.16$ |

The new balance is $413.16.

Think About It

1. The average daily balance is the sum of the daily balances divided by the number of days in a month. Your average daily balance for September (30 days) was $126.20. What was the sum of the daily balances?

_____

☙ ◉ **September** ❧ ❧						
			1	2	3	4
5	6	7	8	9	10	11
12	13	14	15	16	17	18
19	20	21	22	23	24	25
26	27	28	29	30		🎃

Practice

Remember to estimate whenever you use your calculator.

Find the interest on the overdraft checking account.

Sum of daily balances	$2,945	$3,085.00	$4,074	$3,098.45	$2,453.89
Annual percentage rate	19%	20%	17%	18%	17%
Interest	1. _____	2. _____	3. _____	4. _____	5. _____

The Mathematics of Banking and Credit, SV 9780547625614

Name _____ Date _____

Find the interest and the new balance for the account.

6. The sum of the daily balances is $3,485
and the APR is 18%.

Interest: _____

New balance: _____

7. The sum of the daily balances is $7,086
and the APR is 20%.

Interest: _____

New balance: _____

8. Sept. 1: Balance $8.58
Sept. 5: Made $175 payment
Sept. 19: Balance changed to $795
Sept. 20-30: No more activity
The APR is 20%.

Interest: _____

New balance: _____

9. March 1: Balance $908
March 8: Balance changed to $1,035
March 23: Made $295 payment
March 24-31: No more activity
The APR is 18%.

Interest: _____

New balance: _____

10. June 1: Balance $2,085
June 5: Made $475 payment
June 12: Balance changed to $1,985.75
June 23: Balance changed to $2,135.89
June 24-30: No more activity
The APR is 17%.

Interest: _____

New balance: _____

11. July 1: Balance $75
July 9: Balance changed to $525
July 10: Made $175 payment
July 21: Made $75.89 payment
July 22-31: No more activity
The APR is 19%.

Interest: _____

New balance: _____

Remember to estimate whenever you use your calculator.

Use the daily interest rate table in Example 1 on page 92 to find the interest on the overdraft checking account.

Sum of daily balances	$1,987.00	$2,958.39	$3,125.39	$2,560.90	$4,539.80
Annual percentage rate	17%	20%	19%	20%	18%
Interest	**12.** _____	**13.** _____	**14.** _____	**15.** _____	**16.** _____

Sum of daily balances	$3,486.85	$5,795.20	$6,230.60	$7,280.00	$3,709.45
Annual percentage rate	20%	19%	18%	20%	17%
Interest	**17.** _____	**18.** _____	**19.** _____	**20.** _____	**21.** _____

The Mathematics of Banking and Credit, SV 9780547625614

Name _____ Date _____

Find the interest and the new balance for the account.

22. The sum of the daily balances is $4,760 and the APR is 19%.

Interest: _____

New balance: _____

23. The sum of the daily balances is $6,012.55 and the APR is 17%.

Interest: _____

New balance: _____

24. The sum of the daily balances is $589 and the APR is 19%.

Interest: _____

New balance: _____

25. The sum of the daily balances is $763 and the APR is 18%.

Interest: _____

New balance: _____

26. Nov. 1: Balance $438
Nov. 4: Made $182 payment
Nov. 23: Balance changed to $1,342.20
Nov. 24–30: No more activity
The APR is 20%.

Interest: _____

New balance: _____

27. Dec. 1: Balance $1,650
Dec. 12: Balance changed to $930
Dec. 26: Made $305 payment
Dec. 27-31: No more activity
The APR is 17%.

Interest: _____

New balance: _____

28. May 1: Balance $438
May 7: Made $95 payment
May 19: Balance changed to $1,343.50
May 24: Balance changed to $1,906.10
May 25–31: No more activity
The APR is 18%.

Interest: _____

New balance: _____

29. Oct. 1: Balance $65
Oct. 9: Balance changed to $1,386.25
Oct. 21: Made $678.25 payment
Oct. 23: Made $378.75 payment
Oct. 24–31: No more activity
The APR is 20%.

Interest: _____

New balance: _____

30. Jan. 1: Balance $609
Jan. 4: Made $35 payment
Jan. 13: Balance changed to $602
Jan. 20: Balance changed to $699
Jan. 21–31: No more activity
The APR is 17%.

Interest: _____

New balance: _____

31. Feb. 1: Balance $229
Feb. 9: Balance changed to $830
Feb. 16: Balance changed to $975
Feb. 25: Made $675 payment
Feb. 26–28: No more activity
The APR is 19%.

Interest: _____

New balance: _____

Taking Out A Loan

It is wise to apply for different loan rates before you apply for a loan at a certain bank or credit union. The Annual Percentage Rate (APR) is the rate of interest you pay for loans and finance plans.

At a bank or a credit union, a loan officer gives you a loan application to fill out. You usually make monthly payments to pay back a loan.

Example 1: You want to borrow $685 to pay back some debts. The loan officer at a bank tells you that the APR is 13.5%. She also tells you that you will pay off the loan in 12 monthly payments of $61.34. How much will you need to repay? What is the interest?

| **Step 1** | Multiply to find the amount you repay. | $12 \times \$61.34 = \$736.08$ |

You will need to repay $736.08.

| **Step 2** | Subtract to find the interest. | $\$736.08 - \$685.00 = \$51.08$ |

The interest is $51.08.

Banks and credit unions use rate tables to find out how much interest you will pay. The interest depends on the amount borrowed, the interest rate, and how long you will take to repay the loan.

Example 2: Carlos takes out a $600 loan for a vacation trip. The APR is 14.5%. He will repay the loan in 9 months. How much interest will he pay? How much will he repay each month?

THINK: Look across from 9 months in the table to find the interest rate per $100, or $6.138.

INTEREST PER $100	
Month	**14.5 % APR**
3	$2.426
6	$4.315
9	$6.138
12	$8.027
15	$9.937

| **Step 1** | Divide to find the number of $100 that Carlos is borrowing. | $\$600 \div \$100 = 6$ |

| **Step 2** | Multiply to find the interest. | $6 \times \$6.138 = \$36.828$ |

Carlos will pay $36.83 in interest.

| **Step 3** | Add to find the total amount he will repay. | $\$600 + \$36.83 = \$636.83$ |

| **Step 4** | Divide to find the monthly payment. | $\$636.83 \div 9 = \$70.758888$ |

Carlos will repay $70.76 per month for 9 months.

Name _____ Date _____

Banks also use tables to find monthly payments.

Example 3: Victoria got a $7,000 loan to buy a motorcycle. How much will she pay each month for a 10-year loan at $12\frac{1}{4}\%$? How much interest will she pay?

THINK: Look across from 10 years under $12\frac{1}{4}\%$ to find the monthly payment for each $100 borrowed, or $1.499.

MONTHLY PAYMENT PER $100 FINANCED

Years	APR		
	$10\frac{1}{2}\%$	$12\frac{1}{4}\%$	$13\frac{1}{2}\%$
5	2.149	2.237	2.301
10	1.349	1.499	1.523
15	1.105	1.216	1.295

Step 1 Step 1: Divide to find the number of $100. $7,000 ÷ $100 = 70

Step 2 Multiply to find the payment.   70 × $1.499 = $104.93

Victoria will pay $104.93 per month.

Step 3 Multiply to find the total amount to be repaid.

THINK: 10 y = 10 × 12 mo = 120 mo   120 × $104.93 = $12,591.60

Step 4 Subtract to find the interest. $12,591.60 − $7,000 = $5,591.60

Victoria will pay $5,591.60 in interest.

The Mathematics of Banking and Credit, SV 9780547625614

Name _____ Date _____

1. A home equity loan is a **secured loan**, since the value of your home guarantees payment. Would the interest rate on a secured loan usually be more or less than the interest rate on an unsecured loan? Why?

_____

_____

_____

_____

_____

_____

_____

Practice

Remember to estimate whenever you use your calculator.
Find the total amount to be repaid and the interest.

	Amount borrowed	Monthly payment	Number of payments	Amount to be repaid	Interest
1.	$385	$67.31	6	_____	_____
2.	$809	$96.08	9	_____	_____
3.	$580	$52.27	12	_____	_____
4.	$1,200	$75.41	18	_____	_____
5.	$1,385	$104.17	15	_____	_____
6.	$239	$82.13	3	_____	_____

Find the interest and the monthly payment.

INTEREST PER $100

Months	13.5% APR	17.6% APR
3	2.258	2.945
6	3.974	5.192
9	5.705	7.469
12	7.462	9.788
15	9.235	12.131
18	11.026	14.508

Amount Borrowed	APR	Months	Interest	Monthly Payment
$500	13.5%	6	7. _____	8. _____
$750	17.6%	9	9. _____	10. _____
$186	13.5%	3	11. _____	12. _____
$918	13.5%	12	13. _____	14. _____
$1,020	17.6%	12	15. _____	16. _____
$1,860	13.5%	18	17. _____	18. _____
$1,238	17.6%	15	19. _____	20. _____
$908.86	17.6%	18	21. _____	22. _____
$1,087.95	13.5%	15	23. _____	24. _____
$397.85	17.6%	9	25. _____	26. _____

The Mathematics of Banking and Credit, SV 9780547625614

Name _____ Date _____

Find the monthly payment and the interest.

MONTHLY PAYMENT PER $100 FINANCED

Years	APR		
	$11\frac{1}{2}\%$	$13\frac{1}{4}\%$	$15\frac{1}{2}\%$
5	2.199	2.288	2.405
10	1.406	1.508	1.644
15	1.168	1.282	1.433

Amount Borrowed	APR	Years	Monthly Payment	Interest
$6,000	$13\frac{1}{4}\%$	5	27. _____ ;	_____
$8,200	$11\frac{1}{2}\%$	10	28. _____ ;	_____
$9,350	$15\frac{1}{2}\%$	15	29. _____ ;	_____
$8,725	$11\frac{1}{2}\%$	10	30. _____ ;	_____
$11,300	$13\frac{1}{4}\%$	5	31. _____ ;	_____
$9,890	$11\frac{1}{2}\%$	15	32. _____ ;	_____
$13,290	$15\frac{1}{2}\%$	15	33. _____ ;	_____
$6,780	$15\frac{1}{2}\%$	10	34. _____ ;	_____
$18,535	$13\frac{1}{4}\%$	5	35. _____ ;	_____
$23,265	$11\frac{1}{2}\%$	15	36. _____ ;	_____

Find the minimum payment.

37. Kim borrowed $18,565 for 15 years. How much more would her monthly payments have been if the APR were $15\frac{1}{2}\%$ instead of $13\frac{1}{4}\%$?

_____

38. David borrowed $13,675 for 5 years. How much more would he have repaid if the APR were $15\frac{1}{2}\%$ instead of $11\frac{1}{2}\%$?

_____

The Mathematics of Banking and Credit, SV 9780547625614

Name _____ Date _____

Remember to estimate whenever you use your calculator.

Find the total amount to be repaid and the interest.

Amount borrowed	Monthly payment	Number of payments	Total amount to be repaid	Interest
$475	$98.36	5	1. _____	2. _____
$620	$109.53	6	3. _____	4. _____
$785	$92.78	9	5. _____	6. _____
$1,860	$120.38	18	7. _____	8. _____

Using the table on page 99, find the interest and the monthly payment.

Amount borrowed	APR	Months	Interest	Monthly payment
$400	17.6%	3	9. _____	10. _____
$680	13.5%	9	11. _____	12. _____
$375	13.5%	6	13. _____	14. _____
$643	17.6%	12	15. _____	16. _____
$964	13.5%	18	17. _____	18. _____

Use the monthly payment rate table on page 100 to find the monthly payment and the interest.

Amount borrowed	APR	Years	Monthly payment	Interest
$5,000	$15\frac{1}{2}\%$	10	19. _____	20. _____
$7,500	$13\frac{1}{4}\%$	5	21. _____	22. _____
$6,255	$11\frac{1}{2}\%$	15	23. _____	24. _____
$10,120	$13\frac{1}{4}\%$	10	25. _____	26. _____
$9,304	$15\frac{1}{2}\%$	5	27. _____	28. _____

Solve.

29. Vicky borrowed $23,630.00 for 5 y. How much more would her monthly payments have been if the APR were $13\frac{1}{4}\%$ of $11\frac{1}{2}\%$?

_____

30. Geraldo borrowed $9,935.00 for 10 years. How much less would he have repaid if the APR were $11\frac{1}{2}\%$ instead of $15\frac{1}{2}\%$?

_____

Installment Buying

If you want to purchase an expensive item, but do not have enough money to pay for it all at once, you may be able to afford to buy it on an installment plan. An **installment plan** allows you to purchase an item by making payments over time. Some installment plans require a **down payment**, a portion of the sales price, and then allow the buyer to pay for the rest in a series of regular payments. The **installment price** is the total of all of the payments, including the down payment. Installment agreements usually include a **finance charge**, which is the amount you pay to use the installment plan. Typically, an item bought on an installment plan costs more than its regular price. To calculate the finance charge, subtract the regular price from the installment price.

> *$199.50*
> *Installment plans:*
> *$19.15/mo for 12 mo*
> *OR*
> *$30 down, $16/mo for 12 mo*

Finance Charge = Installment Price – Regular Price

Example 1: You choose the installment plan without the down payment. Find the installment price and the finance charge.

| Step 1 | Multiply to find the total monthly payments (the installment price). | $12 \times \$19.15 = \$229.80$ |

The installment price is $229.80.

| Step 2 | Subtract to find the finance charge. | $\$229.80 - \$199.50 = \$30.30$ |

The finance charge is $30.30.

You may choose to pay a down payment when you get your purchase. In this case, the installment price is the total of the **installment payments** and the down payment.

Example 2: Jim chooses the installment plan with the down payment. Find the installment price and the finance charge.

| Step 1 | Multiply to find the total monthly payments. | $12 \times \$16 = \$192.00$ |

| Step 2 | Add to find the installment price. | $\$30 + 192 = \$222.00$ |

The installment price is $222.00.

| Step 3 | Subtract to find the finance charge. | $\$222.00 - \$199.50 = \$22.50$ |

The finance charge is $22.50.

Name _____ Date _____

1. Why did the down payment in Example 2 decrease the finance charge?

_____

_____

2. If the watch were financed for 18 months instead of 12 months, would the monthly payments be more or less? Would the installment price be more or less? Why?

_____

_____

_____

Practice

Remember to estimate whenever you use your calculator.

Find the installment price and the finance charge.

	Regular price	Down payment	Monthly payment	Number of payments	Installment price	Finance Charge
1.	$85.00	$0.00	$15.00	6	_____	_____
2.	$102.00	$0.00	$14.00	9	_____	_____
3.	$198.65	$0.00	$18.00	12	_____	_____
4.	$305.76	$0.00	$27.50	12	_____	_____
5.	$405.00	$80.00	$42.00	9	_____	_____
6.	$598.00	$125.00	$44.00	12	_____	_____
7.	$829.85	$175.00	$80.76	9	_____	_____
8.	$932.96	$245.00	$64.27	12	_____	_____

9. You buy a DVD player on the installment plan. It usually sells for $89.95. You pay $11 per month for 9 months.

_____

10. You buy a television on the installment plan. It usually sells for $439.95. You pay $41 per month for 12 months.

_____

11. The advertisement for a class ring reads, "Nothing down and $17.50 a month for 6 months." The ring usually sells for $89.95.

_____

12. A coat you want is advertised for "$25 down and $35.50 a month for 6 months." The coat usually sells for $220.95.

_____

13. Caroline bought a $425.00 washing machine on an installment plan for $100.00 down and $42.19 per month for a year.

   a. What is the installment price? _____

   b. What is the finance charge? _____

14. Sam wants a car that costs $12,000.00. With a $500.00 down payment, he can buy it on an installment plan paying $201.67 per month for 6 years.

   a. What is the installment price? _____

   b. What is the finance charge? _____

104

| **Extension** | **Annual Percentage Rate (APR)** |

A lender should tell you what the APR is, but you should still figure it out for yourself. It might be more than you think. Use this formula to approximate the APR.

$$\text{Approximate APR} = \frac{24 \times \text{Finance charge}}{\text{Amount financed} \times (\text{Number of payments} + 1)}$$

You need to finance $400 for 12 months toward the cost of a refrigerator. The finance charge is $80. What is the APR?

Step 1 Substitute into the formula. Then solve.

$$\text{APR} = \frac{24 \times 80}{400 \times (12 + 1)} = \frac{\$1,920}{\$400 \times 13} = \frac{\$1,920}{\$5,200} = 0.3692307$$

Step 2 Round to the nearest thousandth and rename as a percent. 0.369=36.9%

The APR is 36.9%.

Find the approximate APR.

Amount Borrowed	Finance Charge	Number of Payments	APR
$400	$20	12	1. _____
$34.86	$2.64	6	2. _____
$375	$21	12	3. _____
$750	$78	18	4. _____
$830	$96.25	15	5. _____
$1,010	$119.50	18	6. _____
$99.95	$2.80	3	7. _____
$65.60	$8.75	9	8. _____

Problem Solving Application: Buying On An Installment Plan

Many stores offer customers different ways to pay for purchases. If you pay for an item all at once, you pay the **cash price**. If you buy the item using a number of payments over a period of time, you are buying the item in **installments**. In this case, the store is providing the credit, and there is a **finance charge** for this service.

You buy a couch and a chair at Helpful Harry's Furniture Company. The cash price of the furniture is $840. You decide to pay in 12 monthly installments. The installments are $76.30 per month. What is the total amount that you pay for the couch and the chair if you use the installment plan? What is the finance charge?

	Number of Installments	×	Amount of Installment		Each Total Amount
1. Multiply to find the total amount.	12	×	$76.30	=	$915.60

	TOTAL	–	CASH PRICE	=	FINANCE CHARGE
2. Subtract the cash price from the total to find the finance charge.	$915.60	–	$840.00	=	$75.60

So, the total amount you pay is $915.60. The finance charge is $75.60.

Name _____ Date _____

Find the total amount and the finance charge.

Cash Price	Number of Installments	Amount of Each Installment	Total Amount	Finance Charge
$480	12	$43.60	1. _____ ;	_____
$720	12	$65.40	2. _____ ;	_____
$540	12	$49.05	3. _____ ;	_____
$1,092	12	$99.19	4. _____ ;	_____
$2,400	24	$120.00	5. _____ ;	_____
$3,600	24	$175.00	6. _____ ;	_____
$5,000	36	$145.02	7. _____ ;	_____
$3,895	48	$109.87	8. _____ ;	_____

Solve.

9. The cash price of dining room furniture is $960. Mrs. Pannier buys it on an installment plan. She pays in 12 monthly installments, $87.20 per month. What is the total amount she pays? What is the finance charge?

_____

10. Doreen Washington buys a stereo system on an installment plan. The total amount of money she pays is $1,194. If each installment is $\frac{1}{6}$ of the total amount, how much is each installment?

_____

11. Pat Chang buys a dining room set on an installment plan. He pays in 12 monthly installments, $71.35 per month. When he has finished paying the installments, the total amount he has paid will be $69.40 more than the cash price. What is the cash price?

_____

Decision Making: Using Credit Wisely

One of the most important decisions you will make is how and when to use credit. You should never borrow money unless you need it. When you do borrow money, choose the credit plan that is best for you.

Problem

To borrow $2,500 for his tuition, Ron can choose one of these credit plans.

- Charge the tuition on his credit card.
- Get an unsecured bank loan.
- Use the school's tuition plan.
- Ask his parents to get a home equity loan, which he will repay.

Ron listed the features of each plan to help him decide.

Credit Card:

Finance charge: $1\frac{1}{2}$% of the unpaid balance each month.

Minimum payment: $100 monthly

The APR is 19.8%.

I plan to make the minimum monthly payment.

I will not charge anything else on this card. It will take me 31 months to pay off the loan. The interest will be $597.52.

School's Tuition Plan:

I can pay the school 12 monthly payments of $220.

The APR is 10.8%.

The loan cannot be paid off any faster.

Unsecured Loan:

The APR is 17.6%

The bank will only give the loan for 18 months.

The loan cannot be paid off any faster.

Home Equity Loan:

The minimum term of the loan is 5 years (60 mo).

The APR is $11\frac{1}{2}$%.

Interest paid is tax deductible.

My parents have the final responsibility for repaying the loan. The loan cannot be paid off any faster.

17.6 % APR Interest Per $100
18 mo........$14.508

$11\frac{1}{2}$% APR Monthly Payment Per $100
5 y........$2.199

Decision-Making Factors

• Annual Percentage Rate	• Monthly payment	• Number of payments
• Interest paid	• Other factors	

Decision-Making Comparisons

Complete the table to compare the 4 credit plans.

Factor	Credit Card	Unsecured loan	School's tuition plan	Home equity loan
APR	1. _____	17.6%	2. _____	3. _____
Monthly payment	4. _____	5. _____	$220.00	6. _____
Number of payments	31	7. _____	8. _____	60
Interest	$597.52	9. _____	10. _____	11. _____
Other factors	12. _____	Payments are fixed	13. _____	14. _____

Making the Decisions

Which account should Victoria open:

15. Lowest APR? _____

16. Lowest monthly payment? _____

17. Least amount of interest? _____

18. Getting a tax deduction? _____

www.harcourtschoolsupply.com
109
Part III
The Mathematics of Banking and Credit, SV 9780547625614

19. Which credit plan would allow Ron to adjust his monthly payments? _____

20. If Ron wants to be totally responsible for repaying the loan, which plan should he eliminate?

_____

21. How much would Ron save in interest by choosing the unsecured loan instead of the home equity loan?

_____

22. How much would Ron save in interest by choosing the school's plan instead of the credit card?

_____

23. Which plans can Ron eliminate if he cannot afford to pay more than $150 per mo?

_____

Of the remaining plans, how much can Ron save by choosing the one with the lowest interest?

_____

24. Should you use APR alone to decide which credit plan to choose? Why or why not?

_____

25. Which one of these credit plans would you choose? Why?

_____

Decision Making: More Practice

Jan needed to borrow $3,600. She listed the features of 3 credit plans to help her decide.

Unsecured Loan   The APR is 13.5%. The loan must be paid off in no more than 15 months. The loan cannot be paid off any faster.

13.5%	Monthly payment per $100
15 months	$9.235

Home Equity Loan   The minimum term of the loan is 5 years (60 mo). The APR is 15.5%. The interest paid is tax deductible. The loan cannot be paid off any faster.

15.5%	Monthly payment per $100
5 years	$2.405

Credit Card   Finance charge: 1.5% of the unpaid balance each month
Minimum payment: $175.83 monthly

The APR is 15.75%. I plan to make the minimum monthly payment. I will not charge anything else on this card. It will take me 24 months to pay off the loan. The interest will be $619.92.

Name _____ Date _____

Complete the table to compare the 3 credit plans.

Factor	Unsecured loan	Home equity loan	Credit Card
APR	1. _____	15.5%	2. _____
Monthly payment	3. _____	4. _____	$175.83
Number of payments	15	5. _____	6. _____
Interest	7. _____	$1,594.80	8. _____
Other factors	9. _____	10. _____	Payments not fixed

Which credit plan would Janice choose if the only factor were:

11. Least amount of interest? _____

12. Lowest monthly payment? _____

Solve.

13. How much would Janice save in interest by choosing the credit card loan instead of the unsecured loan?

_____

14. How much would Janice save in interest by choosing the unsecured loan instead of the home equity loan?

_____

The Mathematics of Banking and Credit, SV 9780547625614

Problem Solving Strategy: Finding a Pattern

Situation:

Ketti has a charge account at the Jaycee Department Store. She used her charge account to buy furniture and began paying for it monthly. With her type of charge account, she can pay a different amount each month. Her finance charges for the first 4 months are shown below.

April	May	June	July
$3.84	$3.68	$3.36	$2.88

Suppose that Ketti makes no other purchases on her charge account and she continues to make payments according to the plan she has been using. What will be the finance charge in August?

Strategy:

Finding a pattern can help you solve some problems.

Applying the Strategy:

The finance charges have been decreasing from one month to the next. Find each difference.

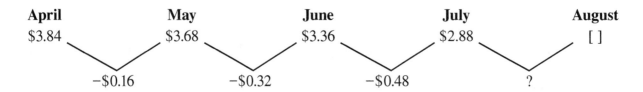

April	May	June	July	August
$3.84	$3.68	$3.36	$2.88	[ ]
−$0.16	−$0.32	−$0.48	?	

Look for a pattern. The differences are increasing by $0.16 each month. The next difference in the pattern will be $0.64, so the finance charge in August will be $2.88 − $0.64, or $2.24.

Practice

Read the problem. Then answer the question. Show your work.

1. Tony's charge account showed unpaid balances as follows: January—$85; February—$110; and March—$135. How did the increase from February to March compare with the increase from January to February?

_____

Solve the problem by finding and using a pattern. Show your work.

2. The finance charges on Beth's charge account were as follows: August—$1.81; September—$1.69; and October—$1.58. If the pattern continues, what will be the finance charge in December?

_____

3. Ari used his charge account to buy audio equipment. With his type of charge account, he can pay a different amount each month. His finance charges for the first 4 months were February—$4.05; March—$3.90; April—$3.60; and May—$3.15. Suppose that Ari makes no other purchases according to the plan he has been using. What will be the finance charge in June?

_____

Name _____ Date _____

4. Helga used her charge account to buy a computer. With her type of charge account, she can pay a different amount each month. Her finance charges for the first 4 months were May—$13.60; June—$11.20; July—$8.80; and August—$6.40. Suppose that Helga makes no other purchases on her charge account and continues to make payments according to the plan she has been using. What will be the finance charge in September?

_____

5. During a 4-month period, Stan kept a record of the unpaid balances on his charge account. The first month, the unpaid balance was $1,000. In each of the other months, the unpaid balance was 1.1 times as great as the unpaid balance the previous month. What were the unpaid balances for the third and fourth months?

_____

6. Luveen kept a record of all her charge account payments for 3 years. The first year, her payments totaled $1,500. In each of the other years, the payments were 80% of those of the previous year. What was the total amount of her payments during the 3 years?

_____

7. Wanda's charge account showed unpaid balances as follows: September—$225; October—$253; and November—$281. If the pattern continues, what will the unpaid balance be in December? How much did the unpaid balance increase each month?

_____

8. Carol uses her charge card to pay her hotel bill. With her type of charge account, she can pay a different amount each month. Her finance charges for the first four months were: January—$9.84; February—$9.45; March—$9.06; and April—$8.67. Suppose Carol makes no other purchases on her charge account and continues to make payments according to the plan she has been using. What will the finance charge be in May?

_____

9. Jonathan uses his charge card to buy airline tickets. With his type of charge account, he can pay a different amount each month. His finance charges for the first four months were: August—$5.40; September—$5.13; October—$4.76; and November—$4.29. Suppose Jonathan makes no other purchases on his charge account and continues to make payments according to the plan he has been using. What will the finance charge be in December?

_____

10. During a 4-month period, Spencer kept a record of the unpaid balances on his charge account. The first month the unpaid balance was $2,250. In each of the other months, the unpaid balance was 1.2 times as great as the unpaid balance the previous month. What were the unpaid balances for the third and fourth months?

_____

Name _____ Date _____

Money Tips 2

By calculating how much credit fits into your budget, you can avoid getting into debt.

Let's Look At The Facts

Charging purchases can be very tempting. It can, however, cause you to spend far beyond your means. The formula below is an easy way to figure out exactly how much you can buy on credit and pay back without getting deeper into debt. Imagine that the budget shown below is yours.

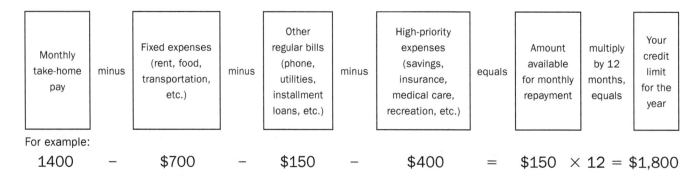

For example:

$$1400 \quad - \quad \$700 \quad - \quad \$150 \quad - \quad \$400 \quad = \quad \$150 \times 12 = \$1,800$$

Let's Discuss Why

1. If your monthly take-home pay is $1,400, what is your annual take-home pay?

   _____

2. What percent of your annual take-home pay does an $1,800 credit limit represent?

   _____

3. What percent of your monthly take-home pay is used for:

   a. Fixed expenses? _____

   b. Regular bills? _____

   c. High-priority expenses? _____

   d. Monthly credit repayment? _____

The Mathematics of Banking and Credit, SV 9780547625614

Name _____ Date _____

Let's See What You Would Do

4. Finance charges (which can range from 12% to 20% or more) are added to the amount you owe on a credit card and are compounded each month. Name some ways to lessen your credit debt.

_____

_____

_____

5. Your rent goes up by $50, raising your fixed expenses to $750. Where could you cut back on spending to make up for this increase?

_____

6. In August, you see a terrific stereo system with a color chamber that changes colors as the music changes. It is on sale for $600 until the end of the year. However, you only have $300 left on your credit limit. Is there any way you could buy it without exceeding your credit limit or borrowing money from anyone?

_____

_____

_____

7. Many experts say that, as a general rule, no more than about 10% to 11% of your take-home pay should be used for buying on credit. If your monthly take-home pay is $1,400, what is your monthly credit range? What is your annual credit range?

_____

_____

_____

Calculator: Percent on a Calculator

You can use a calculator to find what percent one number is of another. Remember, on some calculators you may need to enter the [=] key after the [%] key.

60 is what percent of 75?

Procedure	Calculator Entry	Calculator Display
1. Enter 60.	⑥ ⓪	60.
2. Enter the ➗ key.	➗	60.
3. Enter 75 and the ⑨ key.	⑦ ⑤ ⑨	80.

So, 60 is 80% of 75.

If your calculator does not have a [%] key, multiply by 100 instead.

90 is what percent of 40?

Procedure	Calculator Entry	Calculator Display
1. Divide 90 by 40.	⑨ ⓪ ➗ ④ ⓪ ⌸ ↑ Get ready to divide.	2.25
2. Multiply by 100.	✕ ① ⓪ ⓪ ⌸	225

So, 90 is 225% of 40.

> **TIP** The **CE** key **(Clear Entry)** can help you when you have entered a wrong number into the calculator.

The Mathematics of Banking and Credit, SV 9780547625614

Name _____ Date _____

Use a calculator to find the answers.

1. 45 is what percent of 90? _____

2. 5 is what percent of 20? _____

3. 250 is what percent of 50? _____

4. 110 is what percent of 550? _____

5. 27 is what percent of 0.45? _____

6. $68.40 is what percent of $22.80? _____

7. $3.25 is what percent of $125? _____

8. $18.60 is what percent of $2.50? _____

Use a calculator to solve.

9. Julio earns $1,200 per month. He pays $600 room rent. What percentage of his monthly pay goes for rent?

_____

10. Sally has budgeted $480 for travel expenses. She has already spent $60. What percent has she spent?

_____

11. Frank saved $2.25 of each $25 he earned. What percent of his income did he save?

_____

12. Of 25 students enrolled in a course, 4 transferred out. What percent of the students remained in the course?

_____

Part III
The Mathematics of Banking and Credit, SV 9780547625614

Estimation Skills: Front-End Estimation of Differences

One way to estimate differences is by using front-end estimation.

| **Step 1** | Find the greatest number. |

| **Step 2** | Identify the place of its leading nonzero digit. |

| **Step 3** | Subtract only the digits in that place. |

Examples:

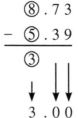

Examples:

$$8.73$$
$$- 5.39$$

③ ↓ ↓↓

Estimate: 3 . 0 0

Examples:

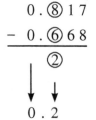

To get a more precise estimate, front-end estimation can be adjusted upward or downward by *also* using the next greatest place. With subtraction, you will need to think of either a *plus* or a *minus* of your next estimate.

Examples:

② 8 , 3 7 2
− 3 , 4 8 0

First estimate: ② 0 , 0 0 0

+ about   5 , 0 0 0

Final estimate: 2 5 , 0 0 0

Examples:

8 . 7 3
− 5 . 3 9

First estimate: ③ . 0 0

+ about   0 . 4 0

Final estimate: 3 . 4 0

Examples:

0 . 8 1 7
− 0 . 6 6 8

First estimate: 0 . ② 0

− about   0 . 0 5

Final estimate: 0 . 1 5

The Mathematics of Banking and Credit, SV 9780547625614

Name _____   Date _____

Use front-end estimation with adjusting to estimate the difference.

1. 573
    − 128

2. 4,309
    − 186

3. 86,245
    − 5,017

4. 33,423
    − 18,507

5. 95,880
    − 8,141

6. 35,081
    − 6,327

7. 24,973
    − 8,789

8. $4.52
    − 3.27

9. $27.50
    − 2.89

10. $9.93
    − 0.50

11. $62.85
    − 37.44

12. $53.75
    − 47.36

13. $47.23
    − 9.72

14. $8.75
    − 0.29

15. $2.09
    − 0.45

16. 6.583
    − 4.471

17. 0.489
    − 0.273

18. 0.892
    − 0.049

19. 0.607
    − 0.152

20. 0.322
    − 0.076

21. 0.873
    − 0.425

22. 0.982
    − 0.079

23. 0.902
    − 0.353

24. 0.513
    − 0.36

The Mathematics of Banking and Credit, SV 9780547625614

Part III Review

Vocabulary

Choose the letter of the word(s) that completes the sentence.

1. On a credit card statement, the _____ is any of the last balance that was not paid.

   a. Finance charge   **b.** New balance   **c.** Unpaid balance

2. A check written for more than the balance in your account is called _____.

   a. A payment   **b.** The daily interest rate   **c.** An overdraft

3. If you cannot afford the full price of an item, you may be able to use _____.

   a. An installment plan   **b.** An APR   **c.** A minimum payment

Skills

Find the unpaid balance, the finance charge, and the new balance.

4. Last balance: $106.84
   Payments: $75.00
   Finance rate: $1\frac{1}{2}\%$
   New charges: $56.28

   Unpaid balance: _____

   Finance charge: _____

   New balance: _____

5. Last balance: $318.60
   Payments: $80.00
   Finance rate: 1.65%
   New charges: $76.39

   Unpaid balance: _____

   Finance charge: _____

   New balance: _____

6. Last balance: $1,100
   Payments: $100
   Finance rate: $1\frac{1}{2}\%$ on first $500
   1% on over $500
   New charges: $65.40

   Unpaid balance: _____

   Finance charge: _____

   New balance: _____

7. Last balance: $850.68
   Payments: $25.00
   Finance rate: $1\frac{1}{2}\%$ on first $500
   1% on over $500
   New charges: $138.75

   Unpaid balance: _____

   Finance charge: _____

   New balance: _____

The Mathematics of Banking and Credit, SV 9780547625614

Name _____ Date _____

Find the interest on the overdraft checking account to the nearest cent.

8. Sum of daily balances: $525
   Daily interest rate: 0.05205%

   _____

9. Sum of daily balances: $2,600
   Daily interest rate: 0.04931%

   _____

Use the loan monthly payment table on page 97 for Exercises 10–13.

10. Sue borrowed $8,000 for 10 years at $13\frac{1}{2}$%. What is the monthly payment? _____

11. May borrowed $14,000 for 10 years at $12\frac{1}{4}$%. What is the monthly payment? _____

12. Dan borrowed $32,600 for 10 years at $13\frac{1}{2}$%. How much interest will he pay? _____

13. Sal borrowed $50,000 for 15 years at $10\frac{1}{2}$%. How much interest will he pay? _____

14. Regular price: $130
    Down payment: $0
    Monthly payment: $17.30
    Number of payments: 9

    Installment price: _____

    Finance charge: _____

15. Regular price: $950.75
    Down payment: $150
    Monthly payment: $88.10
    Number of payments: 12

    Installment price: _____

    Finance charge: _____

Part III Test

Find the finance charge and the new balance.

1. Last balance: $409.56
   Payments: $160.00
   Finance rate: 1.5%
   New charges: $350.49

   Finance charge: _____

   New balance: _____

2. Last balance: $65.43
   Payments: $20.00
   Finance rate: 1.25%
   New charges: $87.60

   Finance charge: _____

   New balance: _____

3. Last balance: $375.00
   Payments: $85.00
   Finance rate: 1.5%
   New charges: $94.00

   Finance charge: _____

   New balance: _____

Use the daily interest rate table on page 92 to find the interest on the account to the nearest cent.

Sum of daily balances	APR	Interest
$270.00	17%	**4.** _____
$456.90	20%	**5.** _____
$509.00	20%	**6.** _____
$810.00	17%	**7.** _____
$3,895.67	17%	**8.** _____
$9,007.62	20%	**9.** _____

Use the table on page 97.

10. Borrowed $500 for 5 years at $10\frac{1}{2}\%$

    Monthly payment: _____

    Total amount to be repaid: _____

    Interest paid: _____

11. Borrowed $9,000 for 10 years at at $10\frac{1}{2}\%$

    Monthly payment: _____

    Total amount to be repaid: _____

    Interest paid: _____

12. Borrowed $4,675 for 10 years at $12\frac{1}{4}\%$

Monthly payment: _____

Total amount to be repaid: _____

Interest paid: _____

13. Borrowed $12,500 for 5 years at at $13\frac{1}{2}\%$

Monthly payment: _____

Total amount to be repaid: _____

Interest paid: _____

Find the installment price and the finance charge.

	mp3 player	DVD player	Microwave oven	Vacuum cleaner
Regular price	$75	$98.89	$210	$273.60
Down payment	$0	$0	$25	$85
Monthly payment	$10.42	$16.75	$17.58	$23.25
Number of payments	9	6	12	9
Installment price	14. _____	16. _____	18. _____	20. _____
Finance charge	15. _____	17. _____	19. _____	21. _____

Your charge account finance charges for the first four months on a single purchase were: January—$8.50; February—$7.55; March—$6.84; and April—$6.37.

22. By how much are the differences in finance charges decreasing each month? _____

23. What is the total difference over the four-month period? _____

24. What should May's finance charge be? _____

Support Materials

Support Materials:
Group Projects

Group Project: Banking and Budgeting

Bill and Jean Smith are a working couple. They want to open a checking account and a savings account at a bank. Bill gets a paycheck of $400 every 2 weeks. Jean gets a paycheck of $350 on the 15th and the end of the month. The couple's $600 rent and $200 auto loan are due on the 15th. The remaining bills are due at the end of the month. Their total monthly expenditures amount to about $1,185. Where would you recommend that the Smiths open their checking and savings accounts? How should the Smiths allocate their earnings in the accounts so they can pay their bills on time and still save $3,000 per year?

Questions to Think About

1. What bank or banks best suit the Smiths?

2. How much should the Smiths deposit in each account each month?

3. When should the deposits be made?

What other questions do you have to think about? Make a list of these questions.

Answering the Questions

Discuss what information you need to answer the first question.

- Investigate some banks for the Smiths. Find out about interest rates, penalties, minimum balances, and so on.

- Summarize the information you collect about each bank in a table or chart. This will help you see the information at a glance.

Answer all the questions in your list.

Formulating and Implementing the Plan

Organize all the information you have gathered.

- Recommend where the Smiths should open their accounts.

- Show what their checking and savings accounts might look like at the end of a given month. Compute all interest due them for each account.

- Present your recommendation to the class. Be prepared to support your recommendation.

Name _____ Date _____

Group Project: Credit Cards

The credit cards issued by the 4 banks listed below were rated best in the category of standard credit cards by a credit card rating service.

Best Credit Cards

Interest Issuer	Annual rate %	Type of fee	Type of card	Grace period
Independence Savings	19.8	Free	Metro	25 days
People's Bank	12.5	$20	Metro and Executive Card	25 days
Manfacture's Bank	14.2	Free	Executive Card	None
Intergrated Savings	14.0	Free	Executive Card	25 days

Terms to Think About

Before you begin, be sure you understand the terms commonly used with credit cards.

- If you are a person who uses a credit card about 6 times per year, you are considered an average user.

- If you use a credit card frequently, in place of carrying cash or writing a check, you are a convenience user.

Be sure you know the meanings of the terms in the chart above.

Analyzing the Cards

With the credit cards on the previous page, you have the option of either paying the monthly minimum specified on your bill or paying in full. Keep this in mind as you discuss the following situations with your group. Decide which card is best for each situation.

- You are an average user who usually pays in full.

- You are a convenience user who usually pays only the monthly minimum.

- You are a convenience user who sometimes pays in full.

Share your decisions with the class. Support your decisions by explaining how the interest rate, annual fee, and grace period affected your decision in each situation.

NOTES:

_____

_____

_____

_____

_____

_____

_____

_____

_____

_____

_____

_____

_____

_____

_____

_____

_____

_____

_____

_____

_____

_____

Support Materials:
Practice Forms

Blank Checks

YOUR NAME

885

DATE   51-57/119

PAY TO THE
ORDER OF _____ | $

_____ DOLLARS

MAPLEWOOD BANK

MEMO _____   _____

⑈011900671⑈   976346 0⑞ 0880

YOUR NAME

885

DATE   51-57/119

PAY TO THE
ORDER OF _____ | $

_____ DOLLARS

MAPLEWOOD BANK

MEMO _____   _____

⑈011900671⑈   976346 0⑞ 0880

YOUR NAME

885

DATE   51-57/119

PAY TO THE
ORDER OF _____ | $

_____ DOLLARS

MAPLEWOOD BANK

MEMO _____   _____

⑈011900671⑈   976346 0⑞ 0880

YOUR NAME

885

DATE   51-57/119

PAY TO THE
ORDER OF _____ | $

_____ DOLLARS

MAPLEWOOD BANK

MEMO _____   _____

⑈011900671⑈   976346 0⑞ 0880

The Mathematics of Banking and Credit, SV 9780547625614

Blank Checking Account Deposit Slips

DEPOSIT TICKET

YOUR NAME

DATE _____

MAPLEWOOD BANK

976346॥▪

CASH		
LIST CHECKS SINGLY		
TOTAL FROM OTHER SIDE		
TOTAL ITEMS	**TOTAL**	

51-57/119

USE OTHER SIDE FOR ADDITIONAL LISTING
◀ ENTER TOTAL HERE

BE SURE EACH ITEM IS PROPERLY ENDORSED

CHECKS AND OTHER ITEMS ARE RECEIVED FOR DEPOSIT SUBJECT TO THE PROVISIONS OF THE UNIFORM COMMERCIAL CODE OR ANY APPLICABLE COLLECTION AGREEMENT

DEPOSIT TICKET

YOUR NAME

DATE _____

MAPLEWOOD BANK

976346॥▪

CASH		
LIST CHECKS SINGLY		
TOTAL FROM OTHER SIDE		
TOTAL ITEMS	**TOTAL**	

51-57/119

USE OTHER SIDE FOR ADDITIONAL LISTING
◀ ENTER TOTAL HERE

BE SURE EACH ITEM IS PROPERLY ENDORSED

CHECKS AND OTHER ITEMS ARE RECEIVED FOR DEPOSIT SUBJECT TO THE PROVISIONS OF THE UNIFORM COMMERCIAL CODE OR ANY APPLICABLE COLLECTION AGREEMENT

DEPOSIT TICKET

YOUR NAME

DATE _____

MAPLEWOOD BANK

976346॥▪

CASH		
LIST CHECKS SINGLY		
TOTAL FROM OTHER SIDE		
TOTAL ITEMS	**TOTAL**	

51-57/119

USE OTHER SIDE FOR ADDITIONAL LISTING
◀ ENTER TOTAL HERE

BE SURE EACH ITEM IS PROPERLY ENDORSED

CHECKS AND OTHER ITEMS ARE RECEIVED FOR DEPOSIT SUBJECT TO THE PROVISIONS OF THE UNIFORM COMMERCIAL CODE OR ANY APPLICABLE COLLECTION AGREEMENT

DEPOSIT TICKET

YOUR NAME

DATE _____

MAPLEWOOD BANK

976346॥▪

CASH		
LIST CHECKS SINGLY		
TOTAL FROM OTHER SIDE		
TOTAL ITEMS	**TOTAL**	

51-57/119

USE OTHER SIDE FOR ADDITIONAL LISTING
◀ ENTER TOTAL HERE

BE SURE EACH ITEM IS PROPERLY ENDORSED

CHECKS AND OTHER ITEMS ARE RECEIVED FOR DEPOSIT SUBJECT TO THE PROVISIONS OF THE UNIFORM COMMERCIAL CODE OR ANY APPLICABLE COLLECTION AGREEMENT

Support Materials
The Mathematics of Banking and Credit, SV 9780547625614

Blank Check Registers

RECORD ALL CHARGES OR CREDITS THAT AFFECT YOUR ACCOUNT

NUMBER	DATE	DESCRIPTION OF TRANSACTION	PAYMENT/DEBIT (−)	✔ T	FEE (IF ANY) (−)	DEPOSIT/CREDIT (+)	BALANCE	
			$		$	$		

RECORD ALL CHARGES OR CREDITS THAT AFFECT YOUR ACCOUNT

NUMBER	DATE	DESCRIPTION OF TRANSACTION	PAYMENT/DEBIT (−)	✔ T	FEE (IF ANY) (−)	DEPOSIT/CREDIT (+)	BALANCE	
			$		$	$		

Support Materials
The Mathematics of Banking and Credit, SV 9780547625614

Blank Savings Account Deposit Slips

SAVINGS DEPOSIT
MAPLEWOOD BANK

OFFICE OF ACCOUNT

DATE

PRINT NAME(S)

ACCOUNT NUMBER

1-0522 2 89[76616]   DO NOT WRITE BELOW THIS LINE

⑆9040⑈0000⑆

	DOLLARS	CENTS
BILLS		
COINS		
CHECK NO.		
TOTAL ▶		

SAVINGS DEPOSIT
MAPLEWOOD BANK

OFFICE OF ACCOUNT

DATE

PRINT NAME(S)

ACCOUNT NUMBER

1-0522 2 89[76616]   DO NOT WRITE BELOW THIS LINE

⑆9040⑈0000⑆

	DOLLARS	CENTS
BILLS		
COINS		
CHECK NO.		
TOTAL ▶		

SAVINGS DEPOSIT
MAPLEWOOD BANK

OFFICE OF ACCOUNT

DATE

PRINT NAME(S)

ACCOUNT NUMBER

1-0522 2 89[76616]   DO NOT WRITE BELOW THIS LINE

⑆9040⑈0000⑆

	DOLLARS	CENTS
BILLS		
COINS		
CHECK NO.		
TOTAL ▶		

SAVINGS DEPOSIT
MAPLEWOOD BANK

OFFICE OF ACCOUNT

DATE

PRINT NAME(S)

ACCOUNT NUMBER

1 0522 2 89[76616]   DO NOT WRITE BELOW THIS LINE

⑆9040⑈0000⑆

	DOLLARS	CENTS
BILLS		
COINS		
CHECK NO.		
TOTAL ▶		

The Mathematics of Banking and Credit, SV 9780547625614

Blank Savings Account Withdrawal Slips

SAVINGS WITHDRAWAL
MAPLEWOOD BANK

	DATE		
		DOLLARS	CENTS
OFFICE OF ACCOUNT	PAY TO MYSELF OR BEARER	$	
			DOLLARS
PRINT ACCOUNT NAME			
ACCOUNT NUMBER	SIGNATURE		

1-0522 2 89[76616]   DO NOT WRITE BELOW THIS LINE

⑈9040⑈0000⑈

SAVINGS WITHDRAWAL
MAPLEWOOD BANK

	DATE		
		DOLLARS	CENTS
OFFICE OF ACCOUNT	PAY TO MYSELF OR BEARER	$	
			DOLLARS
PRINT ACCOUNT NAME			
ACCOUNT NUMBER	SIGNATURE		

1-0522 2 89[76616]   DO NOT WRITE BELOW THIS LINE

⑈9040⑈0000⑈

SAVINGS WITHDRAWAL
MAPLEWOOD BANK

	DATE		
		DOLLARS	CENTS
OFFICE OF ACCOUNT	PAY TO MYSELF OR BEARER	$	
			DOLLARS
PRINT ACCOUNT NAME			
ACCOUNT NUMBER	SIGNATURE		

1-0522 2 89[76616]   DO NOT WRITE BELOW THIS LINE

⑈9040⑈0000⑈

SAVINGS WITHDRAWAL
MAPLEWOOD BANK

	DATE		
		DOLLARS	CENTS
OFFICE OF ACCOUNT	PAY TO MYSELF OR BEARER	$	
			DOLLARS
PRINT ACCOUNT NAME			
ACCOUNT NUMBER	SIGNATURE		

1-0522 2 89[76616]   DO NOT WRITE BELOW THIS LINE

⑈9040⑈0000⑈

The Mathematics of Banking and Credit, SV 9780547625614

Blank Loan Application

WHAT TYPE OF LOAN WOULD YOU LIKE? □ Car □ Home Improvement □ Personal

Amount Requested _____

Number of Repayment Months _____

I would like a □ Fixed Rate Loan □ Variable Rate Loan

PLEASE TELL US ABOUT YOURSELF.

□ Mr. □ Mrs. □ Miss □ Ms _____

<table>
<tr><td></td><td>Last Name</td><td>First</td></tr>
</table>

_____ _____
Date of Birth   Address

□ Own Home   _____
                                                    Telephone No.

□ Rent   _____
                                              Social Security No.

_____
Name and address of Relative not living with you

PLEASE PROVIDE US WITH YOUR EMPLOYMENT HISTORY.

_____ _____
Name of Business Employer   Address

_____ _____ _____
Annual Salary   How Long?   Position

_____
Name of Previous Employer (if less than 2 y at present job)

PLEASE LIST ALL YOUR FINANCIAL OBLIGATIONS.

Please list all loans, credit lines, and credit cards.

Loans

Creditor and Address   Account No.   Balance

_____

_____

_____

WHERE DO YOU BANK?

_____
Checking Account (Bank Name and Address)

_____
Bank Account or Money Market Fund

AGREEMENT

The information above is true and complete.

_____ _____
Applicant's Signature   Date

Support Materials:
Charts and Forms

Simple Interest

Simple interest is generally what people think of when, for instance, they consider paying back a small, personal loan "with interest." It is calculated using a simple formula ($p \times r \times t$), and its gains are moderate. Here is a sample table showing the simple interest on a sum of $1,000 at different rates, over various periods.

Showing the interest on $1,000 at various rates.

Days	2.5%	3.0%	3.5%	4.0%	4.5%	5.0%	5.5%	6.0%	6.5%	7.0%	7.5%	8.0%
1	0.0685	0.0822	0.0959	0.1096	0.1233	0.1370	0.1507	0.1644	0.1781	0.1918	0.2055	0.2192
2	0.1370	0.1644	0.1918	0.2192	0.2466	0.2740	0.3014	0.3288	0.3562	0.3836	0.4110	0.4384
3	0.2055	0.2466	0.2877	0.3288	0.3699	0.4110	0.4521	0.4932	0.5342	0.5753	0.6164	0.6575
4	0.2740	0.3288	0.3836	0.4384	0.4932	0.5479	0.6027	0.6575	0.7123	0.7671	0.8219	0.8767
5	0.3425	0.4110	0.4795	0.5479	0.6164	0.6849	0.7534	0.8219	0.8904	0.9589	1.0274	1.0959
6	0.4110	0.4932	0.5753	0.6575	0.7397	0.8219	0.9041	0.9863	1.0685	1.1507	1.2329	1.3151
7	0.4795	0.5753	0.6712	0.7671	0.8630	0.9589	1.0548	1.1507	1.2466	1.3425	1.4384	1.5342
30	2.0548	2.4658	2.8767	3.2877	3.6986	4.1096	4.5205	4.9315	5.3425	5.7534	6.1644	6.5753
31	2.1233	2.5479	2.9726	3.3973	3.8219	4.2466	4.6712	5.0959	5.5205	5.9452	6.3699	6.7945
90	6.1644	7.3973	8.6301	9.8630	11.0959	12.3288	13.5616	14.7945	16.0274	17.2603	18.4932	19.7260
180	12.3288	14.7945	17.2603	19.7260	22.1918	24.6575	27.1233	29.5890	32.0548	34.5205	36.9863	39.4521
360	24.6575	29.5890	34.5205	39.4521	44.3836	49.3151	54.2466	59.1781	64.1096	69.0411	73.9726	78.9041
365	25.0000	30.0000	35.0000	40.0000	45.0000	50.0000	55.0000	60.0000	65.0000	70.0000	75.0000	80.0000

Compound Interest

Compound interest calculations are not as easy to grasp as are simple interest calculations, because they are actually *series* of calculations—that is, with every period, interest is added, and the *result* becomes the input for computing the interest and the new balance. Here is a table showing what happens to a deposited sum of $100 over a period of years, when its interest is compounded once a year:

Year #	Beginning-of-year value	Rate	Earned interest	End-of-year value *(after Compounding)*
1	$100	10%	$10	$110
2	$110	10%	$11	$121
3	$121	10%	$12.10	$133.10
4	$133.10	10%	$13.31	$146.41
5	$146.41	10%	$14.64	$161.05
6	$161.05	10%	$16.11	$177.16
7	$177.16	10%	$17.72	$194.88
8	$194.88	10%	$19.49	$214.37
9	$214.37	10%	$21.44	$235.81
10	$235.81	10%	$23.58	$259.39

As time goes on, or, if the number of periods is increased, maintaining tables become more time-consuming and less accurate. The chart on page 141 shows the amount of interest gained at various interest rates, with various rates of compounding.

As the situation becomes more complicated, a computer will help you keep track of compound interest.

The Mathematics of Banking and Credit, SV 9780547625614

Compound Interest

Compound Interest Table

No. of Periods	0.5%	1%	1.5%	2%	2.5%	3%	3.5%	4%	4.5%	5%
1	1.0050	1.0100	1.0150	1.0200	1.0250	1.0300	1.0350	1.0400	1.0450	1.0500
2	1.0100	1.0201	1.0302	1.0404	1.0506	1.0609	1.0712	1.0816	1.0920	1.1025
3	1.0151	1.0303	1.0457	1.0612	1.0769	1.0927	1.1087	1.1248	1.1412	1.1576
4	1.0202	1.0406	1.0614	1.0824	1.1038	1.1255	1.1475	1.1699	1.1925	1.2155
5	1.0253	1.0510	1.0773	1.1041	1.1314	1.1593	1.1877	1.2167	1.2462	1.2763
6	1.0304	1.0615	1.0934	1.1262	1.1597	1.1941	1.2293	1.2653	1.3023	1.3401
7	1.0355	1.0721	1.1098	1.1487	1.1887	1.2299	1.2723	1.3159	1.3609	1.4071
8	1.0407	1.0829	1.1265	1.1717	1.2184	1.2668	1.3168	1.3686	1.4221	1.4775
9	1.0459	1.0937	1.1434	1.1951	1.2489	1.3048	1.3629	1.4233	1.4861	1.5513
10	1.0511	1.1046	1.1605	1.2190	1.2801	1.3439	1.4106	1.4802	1.5530	1.6289
11	1.0564	1.1157	1.1779	1.2434	1.3121	1.3842	1.4600	1.5395	1.6229	1.7103
12	1.0617	1.1268	1.1956	1.2682	1.3449	1.4258	1.5111	1.6010	1.6959	1.7959
13	1.0670	1.1381	1.2136	1.2936	1.3785	1.4685	1.5640	1.6651	1.7722	1.8856
14	1.0723	1.1495	1.2318	1.3195	1.4130	1.5126	1.6187	1.7317	1.8519	1.9799
15	1.0777	1.1610	1.2502	1.3459	1.4483	1.5580	1.6753	1.8009	1.9353	2.0789
16	1.0831	1.1726	1.2690	1.3728	1.4845	1.6047	1.7340	1.8730	2.0224	2.1829
17	1.0885	1.1843	1.2880	1.4002	1.5216	1.6528	1.7947	1.9479	2.1134	2.2920
18	1.0939	1.1961	1.3073	1.4282	1.5597	1.7024	1.8575	2.0258	2.2085	2.4066
19	1.0994	1.2081	1.3270	1.4568	1.5987	1.7535	1.9225	2.1068	2.3079	2.5270
20	1.1049	1.2202	1.3469	1.4859	1.6386	1.8061	1.9898	2.1911	2.4117	2.6533
21	1.1104	1.2324	1.3671	1.5157	1.6796	1.8603	2.0594	2.2788	2.5202	2.7860
22	1.1160	1.2447	1.3876	1.5460	1.7216	1.9161	2.1315	2.3699	2.6337	2.9253
23	1.1216	1.2572	1.4084	1.5769	1.7646	1.9736	2.2061	2.4647	2.7522	3.0715
24	1.1272	1.2697	1.4295	1.6084	1.8087	2.0328	2.2833	2.5633	2.8760	3.2251
25	1.1328	1.2824	1.4509	1.6407	1.8539	2.0938	2.3673	2.6658	3.0054	3.3864

Support Materials
The Mathematics of Banking and Credit, SV 9780547625614

Behaviors That Factor Into Your Credit Score

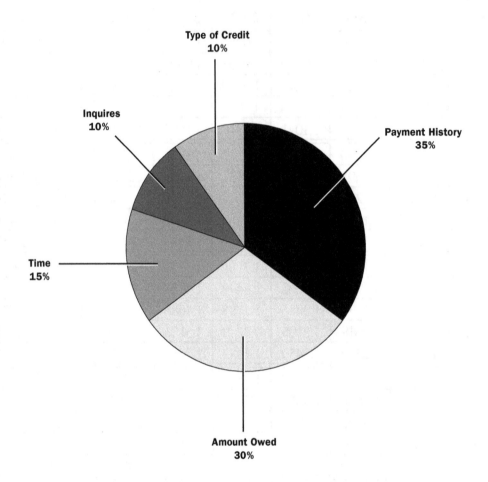

Type of Credit
10%

Inquires
10%

Payment History
35%

Time
15%

Amount Owed
30%

The Mathematics of Banking and Credit, SV 9780547625614

Credit Report Form

CREDIT REPORT — FOR CREDITOR USE

FOR				DATE	TIME OF ISSUE

SUBJECT	SSN	BIRTH DATE
ALSO KNOWN AS		TELEPHONE

CURRENT ADDRESS	DATE REPORTED
FORMER ADDRESS	

CURRENT EMPLOYER AND ADDRESS	POSITION INCOME	VERF	RPTD	HIRE
FORMER EMPLOYER AND ADDRESS				

SPECIAL MESSAGES

_____

_____

_____

_____

CREDIT SUMMARY

PR=1   COL=1   NEG=1   HSTNET=1-6   TRD=2   RVL=1   INST=1   MTG=1   OPN=0   INQ=1

REVOLVING: INSTALLMENT:	HIGH CRED	CRED LIM	BALANCE	PAST DUE	MNTHLY PAY AVAILABLE =
TOTALS					

PUBLIC RECORDS

SOURCE — TYPE	DATE	L1AB		ASSETS	DOCKET # PLAINTIFF/ATTORNEY

COLLECTIONS

SUBNAME ACCOUNT #	SUBCODE	ECOA	OPENED VERIFIED	CLOSED	$ PLACED BALANCE	CREDITOR REMARKS	MOP

Support Materials
The Mathematics of Banking and Credit, SV 9780547625614

What Decides Your Credit Score?

Account Number:		**Current Status:**	PAYS AS AGREED
Account Owner:	Individual Account	**High Credit:**	$0
Type of Account:	Revolving	**Credit Limit:**	$5,260
Term Duration:		**Terms Frequency:**	Monthly (due every month)
Date Opened:	00/0000	**Balance:**	$0
Date Reported:	00/0000	**Amount Past Due:**	$0
Date of Last Payment:		**Actual Payment:**	$0
Scheduled Payment Amount:	$0	**Date of Last Activity:**	00/0000
Date Major Delinquency First Reported:		**Months Reviewed:**	00
Creditor Classification:		**Activity Description:**	
Charge-off Amount:	$0	**Deferred Payment Start Date:**	
Balloon Payment Amount:	$0	**Balloon Payment Date:**	
Date Closed:		**Type of Loan:**	Credit Card
Comments:			

Payment History

Year	Jan	Feb	Mar	Apr	May	Jun	Jul	Aug	Sept	Oct	Nov	Dec
2011	•	•	•	•								
2010	•	•	•	•	•	•	•	•	•	•	•	•
2009	•	•	•	•	•	•	•	•	•	•	•	•
2008	•	•	•	•	•	•	•	•	•	•	•	•
2007	•	•	•	•	•	•	•	•	•	•	•	•
2006	•	•	•	•	•	•	•	•	•	•	•	•
2005	•	•	•	•	•	•	•	•	•	•	•	•
2004	•	•	•	•	•							

Support Materials

The Mathematics of Banking and Credit, SV 9780547625614

Support Materials:
Glossary

Glossary

annual percentage (APR)   A calculation, developed as part of the Truth in Lending Act, that tries to reflect the costs to borrow.

average daily balance   (See **Money Market Checking Account**)

bounce   In banking, describes a situation in which a check is refused by the bank for lack of funds.

cash price   The price of an item if you pay for it in full at time of purchase, as opposed to its price if it is paid for, e.g., in **installments**.

charge receipt   What a merchant issues you as evidence of payment by credit (or charge) card.

checking account   An agreement with a bank that allows the customer to deposit money and write checks against it.

checking account statement   A monthly statement from the bank that lists all changes in a checking account such as deposits, amounts paid by check, service charges, and interest. Checks written by the customer and stamped by the bank, to verify payment, are called **cancelled** checks and were formerly returned to the customer along with the monthly statement. More and more, online checks take the place of handwritten checks, and online banking displays facsimiles of cancelled checks.

compound interest   Interest calculated by periodically (quarterly, or even daily) adding earned interest to an account. The principal then increases more rapidly than with **simple interest**.

credit card   A card that allows the person to whom it is issued to receive purchases and services, but pay for them at a later time. If the entire balance shown on a **monthly statement** is paid by the date due, there is no extra charge. A **minimum payment** is usually required. A **finance charge** is calculated on any **unpaid balance**.

credit card statement   A monthly statement from the bank or credit-issuing company that lists all changes in a credit account such as expenditures, cash advances, amounts paid, finance charges, and interest.

credit union   A cooperative group that makes loans to its members (sometimes a company's employees) at a low rate.

down payment   A portion of the purchase price paid by the customer at time of purchase, to reduce monthly loan payments and to encourage lenders to lend.

estimate   To calculate roughly, when an approximation is sufficient. Used also to check the accuracy of computation.

finance charge   A fee charged for borrowing money, as credit or another type of loan, or for making a purchase in installments.

home equity loan   Money borrowed on the owner's invested value in a house, which serves as security. As is the case with any mortgage, the lender gets the right to take over the house if the loan is not repaid.

installment buying plan   A plan by which the buyer begins using the item purchased at once, but pays for it in periodic **installments**. A **finance charge**, or interest, is added to the **cash price**. If there is a **down payment**, that amount is deducted before the finance charge is figured. The installment price is the total of the installment payments.

installment payment   **installment price** $\times$ number of payments

installment price   total of the **installment payments** and the **down payment**

installments   (See **installment buying plan**.)

interest rate   (See **compound interest; simple interest**.)

loan   Money lent at interest. The interest depends upon the amount borrowed, the interest rate (**Annual Percentage Rate**), and the time it takes to repay the loan.

market value   An approximation of the amount a property could be sold for.

mean   (average) A single number used to represent a set of numbers; found by dividing the sum of the numbers by the number of numbers.

median   The middle value when a set of numbers are listed in order.

mode   The number that occurs most often in a set of numbers.

Money Market checking account   A special checking account that earns interest. To earn interest and to avoid a service charge, most such accounts require that a minimum balance be kept in the account. Interest is usually compounded daily and paid monthly on the basis of the **average daily balance**. Most Money Market accounts limit the number of checks that can be written each month.

new balance   The balance that results after a tally of some kind; i.e., after subtracting outstanding checks from a monthly statement.

online banking   The increasingly common practice of reconciling accounts and/or moving money electronically, via computer.

overdraft   A check written for more than the balance in the account. The bank may lend money to cover overdrafts up to an agreed amount. A **daily interest rate** times the **sum of the daily balances** is the usual way to compute the interest charge on overdrafts. The daily interest rate is based on an **Annual Percentage Rate (APR)**.

percent   A ratio that compares a number to 100. 10 percent (10%) means 10 hundredths, or 10 per 100.

rate   (See **interest rate**.)

reconciled balance   A checking account balance that reflects any changes that are needed to make the bank's monthly statement and the customer's check register agree.

rounding   Replacing a number with an approximation to a nearest given unit, such as to the nearest hundred or tenth. Also, a mixed number can be rounded to the nearest whole number.

savings account   An agreement with a bank whereby a customer deposits money and in return, the bank pays **interest** out of what it earns by investing the money.

secured/unsecured loan   A secured loan is money lent with the understanding that if it is not repaid, some property (house, automobile, furniture) can be taken by the person who made the loan. The property is usually whatever has been bought with the borrowed money. An unsecured loan has the guarantee of the borrower's word that the money will be repaid, but there is no property held as security.

simple interest   A payment for the use of money. The amount of interest depends on the **interest rate** (expressed as an annual percent), on the **principal balance** (the amount of money in the account—or the amount of the mortgage, in the case of various **home equity loans**, for instance), and on the length of time (in years) that the money is used—also referred to as the **term**, in the case of loans.

sum of daily balances   (See **overdraft**.)

unpaid balance   (See **credit card**.)

term   For mortgages and home equity loans, the total number of months that the borrower agrees to pay down the loan—i.e., the "life of the loan."

value checking   A checking account that requires no minimum balance. A very limited number of checks are allowed per month without charge.

Support Materials:
Answer Key

Answer Key

Pages 8-9

Pre-Skills Test

1. 7; 17
2. 9; 8
3. 4; 14
4. 3; 13
5. 8; 18
6. 3; 2
7. 2; 1
8. 3; 13
9. 8
10. 13
11. 15
12. 15
13. 10
14. 12
15. 18
16. 4
17. 4
18. 9
19. 6
20. 2
21. 7
22. 6
23. 4
24. 15
25. 27
26. 36
27. 8
28. 28
29. 42
30. 72
31. 5
32. 9
33. 6
34. 9
35. 6
36. 5
37. 7
38. 6
39. 12
40. 17
41. 18
42. 23
43. 6
44. 48
45. $\frac{5}{14}$
46. $\frac{1}{2}$
47. $\frac{1}{7}$
48. $\frac{6}{7}$
49. 5%
50. 19%
51. 70%
52. 39%
53. 31%
54. 83%

Pages 12-13

Practice

1. 29.8
2. 10,985
3. 82.6
4. 4,819
5. 38.92
6. 21.91
7. 968
8. 36.5
9. 2.94
10. 15 R3
11. 2.23
12. 3.3833
13. 8,497
14. 2,093
15. 43.65

16. 232
17. 37.78
18. 20.69
19. 882
20. 4.25
21. 0.21
22. 15.5
23. 755
24. 4.375
25. 2.6
26. 0.6
27. 0.81
28. 0.82
29. 387 miles
30. $88.45
31. 516 miles
32. $21.08
33. 3,411 miles
34. $375
35. $0.24
36. 363 miles

Pages 16-17

Practice

1. 13%
2. 17%
3. 176%
4. 53%
5. 3.8%
6. 800%
7. 0.5; 50%
8. 0.625; 62.5%
9. 0.8; 80%
10. 2.5; 250%
11. 8.125; 812.5%
12. 4.6; 460%
13. 0.23
14. 0.17

Support Materials
The Mathematics of Banking and Credit, SV 9780547625614

15. 0.03

16. 0.029

17. 0.0006

18. 4.48

19. $\frac{3}{5}$

20. $\frac{3}{10}$

21. $\frac{19}{20}$

22. $1\frac{1}{5}$

23. $1\frac{77}{100}$

24. $2\frac{6}{25}$

25. 2

26. 12

27. 48

28. 3

29. 64.5

30. 21

31. 49

32. 46.5

33. 12

34. 31.5

35. 1.7

36. 31

37. 44 miles

38. 19

39. 16 minutes

40. $10,200

41. $300

42. a. 18

   b. 12

Page 19

Practice

1. 10

2. 10

3. 15

4. 10

5. See student's chart

Page 21

Practice

1. 90

2. 5.1

3. 352

4. 68

5. 14

6. 0.35

7. 14

8. 12

9. 5.6

10. 4.4

11. 4

12. 1.7

13. mean: 75.3; median: 78; mode: none

14. mean: 5.97; median: 5.3; mode: none

15. mean: 337.5; median: 320; mode: 320

16. mean: 75.2; median: 74; mode: 65

17. mean: 4.96; median: 4.2; mode: 2.9

18. mean: 7.55; median: 7.5; mode: 7.5

Extension

1. 21

2. 70, 69

3. 69

4. a. 483

   b. 204

   c. 134

5. 69.24

Page 23

Think About It

1. Answers may vary.

2. Answers may vary.

Practice

1. 936,317

2. 7,817

3. 523

4. 700.481

5. 8,056.503

6. 138.0197

7. 1,600

8. 0.04

9. 21.7

10. 118.1

11. 0.06

12. 0.06

13. 592.539

14. 7.774

15. 17,249 miles

16. 0.0144 cm

Page 25

Think About It

1. Answers may vary.

Practice

1. 59

2. 93

3. 786

4. 69¢

5. $9.50

6. 7.66

7. 41

8. 7

9. 6¢

10. $133

11. $0.89

12. 1.09

13. 380

14. 4.69

15. 12,330

16. 1.34

17. 0.185

18. 29.92

19. $481

20. $235

Extension

1. 3,700

2. 5,750

3. 5,750

Support Materials

The Mathematics of Banking and Credit, SV 9780547625614

Page 27

Think About It
1. Answers may vary.
2. Answers may vary.

Practice
1. 700
2. 1,230
3. $11
4. $6
5. 680
6. 0.5
7. 55,000
8. 0.09
9. 390
10. 20,000
11. $0.10
12. $9
13. 200
14. 7.4
15. $690
16. about $2.00
17. about $100

Page 29

Think About It
1. Answers may vary.

Practice
1. 200,000
2. $400
3. $5,000
4. 320
5. 9
6. 240
7. $240
8. 90
9. 0.09
10. 10
11. 8
12. $2
13. $2

14. $5
15. 10
16. 8
17. 10
18. 30
19. $4.00
20. 3
21. $90
22. 2

Page 31

Think About It
1. Answers may vary.
2. Answers may vary.

Practice
1–6: Answers may vary.
1. mental computation
2. paper and pencil or calculator
3. any of the three
4. calculator
5. 190 miles; calculator or pencil and paper
6. approx. $15.79; calculator or pencil and paper

Pages 32-33

Part I Review
1. a
2. a
3. c
4. 10,604
5. 32.78
6. 1,738
7. 5,707
8. 28.42
9. 21.82
10. 146
11. 728
12. 15.92
13. 469
14. 277

15. 0.35
16. 4%
17. 200%
18. 215%
19. 28%
20. 7%
21. 1.5%
22. 0.78
23. 0.099
24. 3.0
25. 14
26. 4.5
27. 270
28. 9,934
29. 4,097.9922
30. 31.041
31. 35.3934
32. 505
33. 39
34. 2.46
35. 94.223
36. 8,000
37. 9
38. 0.5
39. 15
40. 26
41. 5
42. 10,259 miles
43. 1,070 yards
44. about 53 in.
45. no

Pages 34-35

Part I Test
1. 847
2. 51.17
3. 858
4. 153
5. 2,852
6. 1.82
7. 144

8. 1,953
9. 49.6
10. 532.22
11. 1.3
12. 1.2925
13. 4.76
14. 1.44
15. 0.99
16. 21%
17. 6.6%
18. 20%
19. 175%
20. 12.5%
21. 90%
22. 0.16; 4/25
23. 0.4; 2/5
24. 3.75; 3 3/4
25. 13.6
26. 14
27. 14
28. 9,519
29. 18.14
30. 1,163
31. 36.77
32. 83.5
33. 7.9883
34. 863
35. $1,322
36. 4.54
37. 8
38. $2.02
39. 4,300
40. 7.99
41. 1.1
42. 1.958
43. 1,400
44. 10
45. 1.5
46. $8.50
47. 3,200

48. 10
49. b
50. c
51. $19
52. 1 pack of cards
53. about 10

Part II: Checking and Savings Accounts

Pages 37-38

Pre-Skills Test

1. Forty-eight dollars and seventy-five cents
2. One hundred four dollars and fifty cents
3. Two hundred seventy-nine dollars and thirty cents
4. One thousand, four hundred eighty-three dollars and eighty-nine cents
5. $246.55
6. $474.19
7. $172.47
8. $746.04
9. $85.15
10. $1,837.29
11. $14.65
12. $16.84
13. $6.08
14. $69
15. $6
16. $337.50
17. $363
18. $255.15
19. $384.38
20. $3,525.48
21. 16
22. 13
23. 27
24. 30
25. $7.25

26. $6.40
27. $8.85
28. $10.20

Pages 41-44

Think About It

1. A check "bounces" when there is not enough money in the account to cover it. These days, that amount of funds can be determined instantaneously, by electronic check. Be sure that, at the very moment you write a check, you have enough in your account to cover it.
2. To keep people from tampering with the amount.

Practice

1–8: See student's checks.
9. $160.86
10. $135.16
11. $284.80
12. $326.94
13. $440.23
14. $943.29
15. $384.28
16. $426.53
17. $386.16
18. $267.06
19. $235.82
20. $570.97
21. $69.06
22. $221.13

Pages 46-48

Think About It

1. Cancelled checks serve as records of checking account transactions. They could also be needed for tax purposes.

2. Sometimes you have to maintain a certain minimum balance, or else there is a service charge.

Practice

1. $414.09
2. $398.99
3. 685
4. $19.85
5. $4.75
6. $394.24
7. $476.20
8. $550.43
9. $154.85
10. $247.30
11. $529.79
12. $471.82
13. $521.18
14. $511.08
15. 476
16. $15.60
17. $5.50
18. $505.58

Page 50

Problem Solving Application

1. 425.85
2. 370.60
3. 350.85
4. 401.70
5. 236.38
6. $417.15

Pages 53-56

Think About It

1. Savings accounts are for accumulating money, while checking accounts are for spending money conveniently.
2. Interest is the cost of using money. The bank makes money by lending

your money out at a higher interest rate than it pays you.

Practice

1. $128.29
2. $202.08
3. $272.79
4. $716.15
5. $199.65
6. $333.59
7. $248.94
8. $822.46

9–12: Check completed withdrawal slips.

13. $188.57
14. $41.95
15. $517.12
16. $38.69
17. $2,223.92
18. $222.31
19. $128.85
20. $83.85
21. $56.35
22. $142.71
23. $143.76
24. $79.76
25. $95.60
26. $174.74
27. $59.23
28. $672.68
29. $57.83
30. $840.87
31. $171.89
32. $96.89
33. $120.56
34. $166.06
35. $111.06
36. $113.54
37. $115.06
38. $166.28

39. $495.41
40. $220.09
41. $652.93
42. $1,962.98
43. $550.82
44. $515.82
45. $465.82
46. $671.32
47. $847.20
48. $747.20
49. $807.65

Pages 59-62

Think About It

1. Compounded daily earns more in a year, because principal grows each day, not just once a quarter.
2. Banks profit from the use of your money.

Practice

1. $20; $270
2. $22.50; $522.50
3. $62.50; $1,312.50
4. $1,924.80; $9,944.80
5. $367.50; $3,867.50
6. $212.50; $1,062.50
7. $177.53; $2,807.53
8. $514.06; $6,389.06
9. $20.10; $1,020.10
10. $177.31; $5,177.31
11. $10.09; $410.09
12. $170.34; $7,670.34
13. $4,416.40
14. $6,899.10
15. $10,831.00
16. $4,063.04

Extension

1. They pay interest. They require a minimum balance.
2. $62.50

Practice

1. $63
2. $413
3. $120
4. $720
5. $437.50
6. $1,687.50
7. $972
8. $5,022
9. $3,144
10. $9,694
11. $701.25
12. $3,251.25
13. $712.50
14. $1,662.50
15. $2,121.80
16. $121.80
17. $4,436.83
18. $436.83
19. $535.93
20. $35.93
21. $6,932.92
22. $432.92
23. $3,812.93
24. $312.93
25. $7,354.38
26. $354.38
27. $6,843.00
28. $6,047.55
29. $19,424.40
30. $5,968.71
31. $14,859.00
32. $10,786.50

Pages 63-66

Think About It

1. Banks seek additional accounts because they can invest the money in loans and other types of investments.

Practice

1. $60
2. $112
3. $54
4. $250
5. $562.50
6. $350
7. $371.25
8. $5.00
9. $2,000
10. $96.25
11. $6,000
12. $4,851
13. $56.25
14. $562.50
15. $5,625
16. $56,250
17. $3,744
18. $10.36
19. $1,776.25
20. $217.81
21. $515.15
22. $520.30
23. $525.50
24. $530.76
25. $5,151.69
26. $303.01

Pages 68-70

Decision Making

1. $1,000
2. None
3. $2,000
4. $5.00
5. $7.50
6. $7.50
7. 25¢
8. 20¢
9. 25¢
10. No
11. Yes; 2%
12. No
13. Money Market
14. Regular
15. Value
16. NOW
17. $8.00; $96.00
18. $0
19. $11.25
20. Interest + fee = $156
21. Answers may vary.
22. Answers may vary.
23. $5
24. $1,500
25. 5 withdrawals per month
26. $1\frac{1}{2}$%
27. None
28. $3 per month if balance falls below $1,500
29. Regular savings
30. Money market savings
31. Regular savings
32. Money Market savings
33. $100
34. Answers may vary.

Pages 71-72

Decision Making: More Practice

1. None
2. $1,500
3. $2,500
4. $7.00
5. $6.50
6. $6.50
7. 20¢
8. 20¢
9. 25¢
10. no
11. no
12. yes
13. NOW

14. Money market

15. $0

16. $8.90

17. $8.10; $97.20

18. $169.20

Pages 73-74

Money Tips

1. cash withdrawals, deposits

2. transfer funds, get account information

3. no waiting on long lines, open 24 hours per day, 7 days per week

4. to pay for the ATM service; to cover costs of operation

5. it costs more to give cash; it depletes the bank's funds

6. $144

7. $115.20

8. read your ATM agreement; check your monthly statement; call the bank

9. Pros: Warshaw Bank charges no fees; you may need only 1 ATM location (if your office is also near home); also has an airport ATM, convenient if you do a lot of traveling; however, you lose the flexibility of the large number of ATMs that Capital City Bank has.

10. They could use it to get your money; criminals often know how to use a PIN with a phony ATM card or can manipulate the machine as long as they have a valid PIN with which to work.

Page 76

Calculator

1. 0.625

2. 0.35

3. 0.429

4. 4.6

5. 6.167

6. .75

7. 45%

8. 44%

9. 71.4%

10. 16.7%

11. 360%

12. 948%

13. 656.3%

14. 783.3%

15. 833.3%

16. Sample response:

 ; 37.5%

Pages 77-78

Part II Review

1. b

2. c

3. c

4. $373.77

5. $1,855.73

6. $302.50

7. $541.43

8. $213.99

9. $82.75

10. $112.50

11. $880

12. $33.24

13. $6,734.50

Pages 79–80

Part II Test

1–4. See student's checks.

5. $198.75

6. $152.50

7. $461.07

8. $843.59

9. $79.90

10. $482.85

11. $146.54

12. $73.53

13. $176.56

14. $135.15

15. $90

16. $230

17. $2,707.25

18. $6,629.40

Part III: Credit

Pages 82-83

Pre-Skills Test

1. $27.87

2. $4.92

3. $30.91

4. $86.21

5. $0.08

6. $0.05

7. 0.15

8. 0.53

9. 0.07

10. 0.03

11. 1.05

12. 1.56

13. 0.01

14. 0.015

15. 0.0125

16. 0.000405

17. 0.0006308

18. 0.0005506

19. $36

20. $28

21. $54.60

22. $501

23. $245

24. $437

25. $590.92

26. $635.54

27. $30.77

28. $15.01
29. $59.96
30. $495.09
31. $348.08
32. $212.76
33. $352.71
34. $840.42
35. $30.35
36. $4.46
37. $0.42
38. $0.28
39. $68.67
40. $141.57
41. $76.23
42. $135.49
43. $0.38
44. $0.82
45. $0.02
46. $0.00

Page 86

Think About It

1. Check that all amounts match, that there are no charges on the statement that you did not make, and that any payments are recorded as credits. Keep card receipts!

Practice

1. 123 789 2
2. February 22, 2011
3. June 30, 2011
4. $11.99
5. $2.995
6. AFT-702
7. Feb. 28, 2011
8. 123 789 456 2
9. $158.88
10. $79.39
11. $62.05
12. $1.39

13. $142.93
14. $75.00
15. 21%
16. 18%
17. $9.00
18. $20.45

Pages 89-91

Think About It

1. Examples of advantages: being able to pay for purchases once monthly; having a record of purchases. Examples of disadvantages: It is easy to forget that charging is spending money. It may be easy to exceed what you can afford to repay monthly. Also, there are finance charges when you don't pay your balance in full.

Practice

1. $80.45; $0.80; $181.10
2. $40.55; $0.53; $129.83
3. $43.50; $0.44; $43.94
4. $70.77; $1.06; $71.83
5. $405.85; $4.87; $410.72
6. $159.65; $2.00; $361.54
7. $35.85; $0.54; $382.29
8. $275.63; $2.07; $1,113.95
9. $218.35; $3.28; $257.12
10. $7.95
11. $9.68
12. $17.15
13. $9.29
14. $22.96
15. $234.00; $3.51; $582.51
16. $589.00; $8.39; $597.39
17. $1,784.00; $20.34; $2,038.34
18. $309.79; $4.65; $352.78

Extension

1. $54.72
2. $25

Practice

1. Unpaid balance: $105.20
   Finance charge: $1.32
   New balance: $148.58
2. Unpaid balance: $96.80
   Finance charge: $1.45
   New balance: $211.65
3. Unpaid balance: $72.89
   Finance charge: $1.02
   New balance: $110.90
4. Unpaid balance: $133.20
   Finance charge: $1.60
   New balance: $134.80
5. Unpaid balance: $122.03
   Finance charge: $2.14
   New balance: $335.62
6. Unpaid balance: $371.88
   Finance charge: $4.46
   New balance: $891.14
7. $4.87
8. $9.99
9. $14.53
10. $7.97
11. $28.47

Pages 93-95

Think About It

1. The sum of the daily balances was $3,786.

Practice

1. $1.53
2. $1.69
3. $1.90
4. $1.53
5. $1.14
6. $1.72; $3,846.72
7. $3.88; $7,089.88
8. $12.35; $807.35

9. $14.07; $754.07
10. $27.26; $2,163.15
11. $4.16; $278.27
12. $0.93
13. $1.62
14. $1.63
15. $1.40
16. $2.24
17. $1.91
18. $3.02
19. $3.07
20. $3.99
21. $1.73
22. $2.48; $4,762.48
23. $2.80; $6,015.35
24. $0.31; $589.31
25. $0.38; $763.38
26. $9.27; $1,351.47
27. $16.26; $641.26
28. $14.16; $1,920.26
29. $11.80; $341.30
30. $9.13; $708.13
31. $9.17; $309.17

Pages 98-101

Think About It

1. Interest rates for secured loans are usually less. The bank takes less risk with a secured loan because it has something that it can repossess, if necessary, and sell, to get at least some of its capital back.

Practice

1. $403.86; $18.86
2. $864.72; $55.72
3. $627.24; $47.24
4. $1,357.38; $157.38
5. $1,562.55; $177.55
6. $246.39; $7.39
7. $19.87

8. $86.65
9. $56.02
10. $89.56
11. $4.20
12. $63.40
13. $68.50
14. $82.21
15. $99.84
16. $93.32
17. $205.08
18. $114.73
19. $150.18
20. $92.55
21. $131.86
22. $57.82
23. $100.47
24. $79.23
25. $29.72
26. $47.51
27. $137.28; $2,236.80
28. $115.29; $5,634.80
29. $133.99; $14,768.20
30. $122.67; $5,995.40
31. $258.54; $4,212.40
32. $115.52; $10,903.60
33. $190.45; $20,991.00
34. $111.46; $6,595.20
35. $424.08; $6,909.80
36. $271.74; $25,648.20
37. $28.04
38. $1,690.20

Practice

1. $491.80
2. $16.80
3. $657.18
4. $37.18
5. $835.02
6. $50.02
7. $2,166.84
8. $306.84

9. $11.78
10. $137.26
11. $38.79
12. $79.87
13. $14.90
14. $64.98
15. $62.94
16. $58.83
17. $106.29
18. $59.46
19. $82.20
20. $4,864
21. $171.60
22. $2,796
23. $73.06
24. $6,895.80
25. $152.61
26. $8,193.20
27. $223.76
28. $4,121.60
29. $21.03
30. $2,837.44

Pages 103-105

Think About It

1. Because less money was owed on installment. (However, you cannot assume that the finance charge for one installment plan is less than another plan just because there is a down payment.)

2. The monthly payments would probably be less because there would be more payments. The installment price would probably be more because the money would be paid back over a longer period of time.

Practice
1. $90; $5
2. $126; $24
3. $216; $17.35
4. $330; $24.24
5. $458; $53
6. $653; $55
7. $901.84; $71.99
8. $1,016.24; $83.28
9. $99; $9.05
10. $492; $52.05
11. $105; $15.05
12. $238; $17.05
13. a. $606.28
    b. $181.28
14. a. $15,020.24
    b. $3,020.24

Extension
1. 9.2%
2. 26.0%
3. 10.3%
4. 13.1%
5. 17.4%
6. 14.9%
7. 16.8%
8. 32.0%

Page 107
Problem Solving Application
1. $523.20; $43.20
2. $784.80; $64.80
3. $588.60; $48.60
4. $1,190.28; $98.28
5. $2,880.00; $480.00
6. $4,200.00; $600.00
7. $5,220.72; $220.72
8. $5,273.76; $1,378.76
9. $1,046.40; $86.40
10. $199
11. $786.80

Pages 109-110
Decision Making
1. 19.8%
2. 10.8%
3. $11\frac{1}{2}$%
4. $100.00
5. $159.04
6. $54.98
7. 18
8. 12
9. $362.70
10. $140
11. $798.80
12. Payments not fixed.
13. Payments fixed.
14. Payments fixed; interest tax deductible.
15. School's tuition plan
16. Home equity loan
17. School's tuition plan
18. Home equity loan
19. Credit card
20. Home equity loan
21. $436.10
22. $457.52
23. Unsecured loan, school's tuition plan; $201.28
24. No; reasons may vary
25. Answers may vary.

Page 111
Decision Making: More Practice
1. 13.5%
2. 15.75%
3. $332.46
4. $86.58
5. 60
6. 24
7. $1,386.90
8. $619.92

9. Payments fixed
10. Payments fixed
11. Credit card
12. Home equity
13. $766.98
14. $207.90

Pages 113-115
Problem Solving Strategy
Practice
1. It was the same.
2. $1.48
3. $2.55
4. $4.00
5. $1,210; $1,331
6. $3,660
7. $309; $28
8. $8.28
9. $3.72
10. $3,240; $3,888

Pages 116–117
Money Tips
1. $16,800
2. 10.7%
3. a. 50%
    b. 10.7%
    c. 28.6%
    d. 10.7%
4. Pay your total balance; charge no more than you can afford to pay back in a predetermined amount of time.
5. food, transportation, telephone, recreation
6. Send in a $300 payment instead of the minimum amount on your next monthly statement, or send an additional $75 each month for September through December.

Support Materials
The Mathematics of Banking and Credit, SV 9780547625614

7. Monthly: $140–$154;
Annual: $1,680–$1,848

Page 119

Calculator

1. 50%

2. 25%

3. 500%

4. 20%

5. 6,000%

6. 300%

7. 2.6%

8. 744%

9. 50%

10. 12.5%

11. 9%

12. 84%

Page 121

Estimation Skills

1. 450

2. 4,200

3. 81,000

4. 15,000

5. 87,000

6. 29,000

7. 16,000

8. $1.30

9. $25.00

10. $9.40

11. $25.00

12. $6.00

13. $38.00

14. $8.50

15. $1.60

16. 2.1

17. 0.21

18. 0.85

19. 0.45

20. 0.25

21. 0.45

22. 0.91

23. 0.55

24. 0.15

Pages 122-123

Part III: Review

1. c

2. c

3. a

4. $31.84; $0.48; $88.60

5. $238.60; $3.94; $318.93

6. $1,000; $12.50; $1,077.90

7. $825.68; $10.76; $975.19

8. $0.27

9. $1.28

10. $121.84

11. $209.86

12. $26,979.76

13. $49,450.00

14. $155.70; $25.70

15. $1,207.20; $256.45

Pages 124-125

Part III: Test

1. $3.74; $603.79

2. $0.57; $133.60

3. $4.35; $388.35

4. $0.13

5. $0.25

6. $0.28

7. $0.38

8. $1.81

9. $4.94

10. $10.75; $645; $145

11. $121.41; $14,569.20;
$5,569.20

12. $70.08; $8,409.60;
$3,734.60

13. $287.63; $17,257.80;
$4,757.80

14. $93.78

15. $18.78

16. $100.50

17. $1.61

18. $235.96

19. $25.96

20. $294.25

21. $20.65

22. $0.24

23. $2.13

24. $6.14